THE MANY FACES OF YOGA

SAYALI NAVALKAR

HOW ACADEMICS
an imprint of Highlyy Publishing LLP

ISBN: 978-93-6009-341-9 (Paperback)
First Published : 2024

Published by : HOW ACADEMICS

an imprint of Highlyy Publishing LLP

Correspondence Address : 4/30 A II Floor, Double Storey Buildings
Vijay Nagar, Delhi-110009
Editorial: +91 9811026449
Sales : +91 9999953412
Email: info@howacademics.com
Website: www.howacademics.com

Contents

Preface

Yoga is a science of living. It needs to be incorporated in daily life. It works on physical, mental, emotional, social and spiritual levels of human beings. Yoga helps in improving the quality of life. For example, yoga teaches us how to think, behave and grow to become a fully mature person. Yoga brings harmony between body and mind. It is an art and science for healthy living. The word 'yoga' is derived from the Sanskrit word 'yuj' meaning to join, to yoke, and to unite. It is an ancient system of self-development and natural process of evolution of human beings. Now a days, the word yoga has a strong impact on human life. The ultimate purpose of yoga is the attainment of human growth. Yoga has been established as a new field in education system. It helps in achieving higher state of consciousness on the evolution of an individual's development. It is the discipline of body and mind."Many Faces of Yoga," is a comprehensive exploration that dives into the essence of this ancient practice. From its roots in spirituality to its modern manifestations, this book offers a multifaceted journey through the diverse facets of yoga. In "The Nature of Yoga," discover the foundational principles that underpin this profound discipline, unraveling its essence and purpose. Journey through the rich tapestry of "Schools of Thought," exploring the varied philosophies and approaches that have shaped yoga over centuries. Embark on a scientific exploration of yoga in "Yoga as Science," delving into its physiological and psychological benefits. Then, transition into "Yoga as Practice," where practical techniques and methodologies await, guiding you on your personal journey of transformation. Unlock the power of concentration in "Concentration," as you learn to harness your focus and elevate your practice to new heights. Explore the realms of self-mastery in "Personal Magnetism, Will-Culture, Self-Control," discovering the profound connection between mind, body, and spirit. In "Somaesthetics and Yoga," delve into the aesthetic dimensions of yoga, exploring how movement and expression intertwine with inner awareness. Finally, in "The Yogi Self-Developer," embark on a journey of self-discovery and evolution, as you cultivate the skills and qualities of a true yogi. With its insightful discourse and practical wisdom, "Many Faces of Yoga" invites you to explore the boundless possibilities of this timeless practice, illuminating the path to inner peace, harmony, and self-realization.

Chapter 1
Philosophy of Yoga

In this first talk, we'll try to get a general idea of what Yoga is all about by looking at its place in nature, its own nature, and its role in human growth.

The Universe

Before we do anything else, let's look around and ask ourselves what the past of the world means. What does history tell us when we read it? It looks like a moving picture of people and events, but it's really just a dance of shadows. The kings, statesmen, ministers, and armies are all shadows, not real people. And the battles, uprisings, and rises and falls of states are the most shadowy dance of all. Even if a historian tries to dig deeper by studying things like economic conditions, social structures, and the trends of different schools of thought, he is still in the shadows, the false shadows caused by things that can't be seen. There are a lot of false shapes and values in this world. The proportions and values are all off. A spiritual man must throw away things that a man of the world thinks are important because they are not worth it. The world's diamonds, beautiful as they are when they sparkle in the sun, are just broken glass to a man of understanding. For a person who has seen the beauty of the Self even once, the crown of the king, the sceptre of the emperor, and the victory of worldly power are nothing. So, what is real? What is really worth having? The man of the world will give a very different answer than we will.

"There is a universe because of the Self." The Great Architect plans and builds His worlds not for what the outside world can give, not for power over things people want, and not even for beauty or pleasure. The things he put in them are beautiful and make him happy. The big arch of the sky above, the snow-covered peaks of the mountains, the green, flower-filled valleys, and the seas, with their deep depths and waves that look like lakes sometimes and are rough at other times. All of these things exist not because they are objects, but because they are valuable to the Self. For the Self's sake, and so that His manifestations are possible, not for themselves because they are anything in themselves.

With great creativity, the world is planned so that the powers of the Self can be shown in the real world. The world has beauty, happiness, sorrow, joys, and pains. The fire-mist and the LOGOS are both there for the Self. The tiniest bit of dust, the strongest deva in the heavens, the plant that grows in the corner of a mountain that no one can see, and the star that shines above us are all here so that the parts of the one Self that are manifested in many forms can realise who they are and show the powers of the Self through the matter that surrounds them.

It doesn't matter how high or low you are; there is only one Self. "Mamamsaha" means "my part," and Sri Krishna says that all of these Jivatmas are parts of His own self. For them, the universe exists, the sun shines, the waves roll, the winds blow, and it rains so that the Self can know Himself as made of matter and present in the universe.

Consciousness

One of the deep and important ideas that Theosophy throws around a lot is that the same scale is repeated over and over, with the same series of events happening in circles that are bigger or smaller. You can understand the whole cycle if you know how one cycle works. The rules that govern how a solar system is put together also govern how people are put together. The Self shows off his powers in the universe, from the fire-mist to the LOGOS. These are the same consciousness laws that show up in the world of people. If you understand them in one, you can understand them in the other too. If you hold them in the small, the big will become clear. If you grasp them in the big, you can understand the small.

The big story of how the stone turned into the God goes on for millions of years, aeons. But the long unfolding that happens in the world happens in a shorter time cycle for people. This cycle is so short that it doesn't seem to exist next to the longer one. The same thing happens in the person in an even shorter cycle: quickly, quickly, with all the force of its past behind it. The power of these forces that show up and hide themselves in evolution builds over time. They become a part of the stone and the material world, where they grow and put out a little more strength. This is where they complete their unfolding. Then they get too strong for the element and move on to plants. There, they show more and more of their divinity until they are too strong to be plants and turn into animals.

As they grow inside the animal and learn from it, they again go beyond the limits of the animal and show up as humans. They still grow and build up with more and more force inside a person, putting more pressure on the barrier. Then they push through the human and into the superhuman. The name for this last step in development is "Yoga."

When it comes to the individual, man has evolved over a long period of time in different ways than ours. He has evolved from a mineral to a vegetable, then to an animal, and finally to man. He has also evolved from our last home on the moon to this land-based globe we call earth. Our evolution now has all the power of the last evolution in it. This is why, when we reach this shortest cycle of evolution, which is called Yoga, man has all the forces that have built up during his human evolution behind him. It is this buildup of forces that lets him make the passage so quickly. If we don't connect Yoga to the evolution of consciousness everywhere, we won't understand it at all. This is because the laws of evolution of consciousness in a universe are the same as the laws of yoga. Also, the principles that govern how consciousness unfolds itself in the evolution of humanity are the same principles that we use in yoga to speed up the unfolding of our own consciousness. That means Yoga is not a new thing, as some people think, once it starts.

In its most basic form, evolution is one thing. The order is the same, and the steps are the same. You can study the laws of the whole, whether you're thinking about how consciousness unfolds in the world, in people, or in a single person. In Yoga, you learn how to apply those laws to your own consciousness in a clear and logical way. All rules are the same, even if they show up in different ways at different times.

If you look at Yoga in this way, the strange and faraway thing that seemed to be Yoga will start to look like something you know and not so strange. It won't seem so strange that you can go from being human to superhuman, crossing the line between humanity and reaching the place where divinity is more visible, as you learn more about how awareness grows and how form changes along with it.

Wholeness

Your Self and the Self in everyone else are the same. No matter what skills are shown in the world, they are present in germ, latency, and you. The Supreme does not change. He is the only one who adds or takes away. The Jivatmas, which are parts of Him, are the same as Himself. Their powers only show up in matter when the situations around them make them do so. If you can see how the Self is one in the midst of the Not-Self's many differences, then Yoga won't seem so hard.

Self-discovery

Men and women, you are already smart and thoughtful. You have already climbed that long ladder that separates the form of the Deity in you from His form in the dust. The visible God sleeps in the rock and crystal. He shows Himself more and more in plants and animals, and in people, He has finally reached what most people see as His peak. Since you've already done so much, why not do more? Given how far awareness has come, does it not seem possible that it will continue to grow into the Divine?

There are the same laws that govern the evolution of form and the unfolding of consciousness in the universe and in people. It is through these laws that the yogi brings out his hidden powers. Once you understand this, you will also know that you don't have to go to the mountains, the desert, a cave, or the forest to be united with your Self. He who is inside and outside of you. For certain reasons, privacy may be helpful sometimes. Sometimes it's a good idea to take a break from the busy places where men hang out. Isvara planned the universe so that the powers of the Self could be shown. That is where your best yoga field is, because it was planned with divine knowledge and insight. For that reason, the world is supposed to help the Self grow. So why would you try to escape it? Check out Shri Krishna in the Bhagavad-Gita, which is a very important yoga text. He said it in battle, not on top of a mountain. He said it to a Kshattriya who was ready to fight, not to a Brahmana who was taking it easy and leaving the world behind. The field of yoga is the world's Kurukshetra. Yoga is hard, and people who can't handle the world aren't strong enough to do it. How are you going to deal with the problems in your inner life if the outside world wears you down? How can you hope to get past the problems that yogis have to deal with if you can't get past the little problems that happen in life? These guys are wrong when they think that the only way to win is to run away from the world and that peace can only be found in certain places.

As it turns out, you have done yoga unknowingly in the past, before your self-consciousness had separated itself and became aware of itself. The sand knew it was different from everything else around it, if only for a short time. That is the first thing you should think about and hold on to: yoga is just a sped-up version of the normal development of consciousness.

Once this is done, yoga could be called the "rational application of the laws of the unfolding of consciousness in a single case." That's what it means to use the ways of Yoga. You learn about the rules that govern how consciousness plays out in the world and then use those rules to solve a unique problem: yours. They can't be used on another thing. They have to be put on by yourself. That is the clear idea to understand. We need to add one more word to our definition: "Yoga is the rational application of the laws of the unfolding of consciousness, self-applied in a personal case."

Yoga Is a Science

Next, Yoga is a field of study. That's the second thing you need to understand. Yoga is not just a hazy idea or a dream. It is a science. It is an applied science, which means that it is a set of organised rules that are used to reach a clear goal. The law of psychology is used to explain how the whole awareness of man develops on every level, in every world. These laws are then logically applied to a certain situation. When the rules of unfolding consciousness are used in this way, they work exactly the same way that they are used every day in other areas of science.

You can see how much man's intelligence can speed up "natural" processes by working with nature by looking at the world around you. The way intelligence works is just as "natural" as anything else. There is a real difference between "rational" and "natural" growth because people are smart enough to change the way natural laws work. And when it comes to Yoga, we're in the same area of applied science as a scientific farmer or gardener who uses the natural laws of selection to breed animals. If a farmer or gardener wants to work against the rules of nature, he can't. He only has the universal rules of nature to work with, but he does in a few years what nature might take hundreds of thousands of years to do. How and why? By using human intelligence to pick the rules that help him and get rid of the ones that get in his way. He makes people smart enough to use nature's divine forces, which are working for the good of all instead of just one person.

For example, a pigeon producer will take a blue rock pigeon and turn it into a pouter or a fan-tail. He does this by picking out, generation after generation, the shapes that best show off the trait he wants to develop. He pairs these birds up, looks at all the good conditions, and chooses again and again, until the trait he wants to establish is clearly visible. If you take away his guiding intelligence and leave the birds alone, they will go back to their original type.

Or think about the yard. Every rose in the yard comes from the wild rose of the hedge. The many-petalled rose is just a scientifically improved version of the wild five-petalled rose that grows in hedgerows. Bees and flies do the same thing every day when they pick pollen from one plant and put it on the fruit of another plant. This is what a farmer does on purpose. But he picks his plants carefully. He picks the ones whose qualities he wants to bring out even more. Then he picks the ones whose qualities he wants to bring out even more clearly. This continues until he has made a flower that is so different from the original stock that you can only tell which stock it came from by following its roots.

This is also true in the way that the rules of psychology are used in what we call Yoga. Yoga is the systematic study of how awareness unfolds and how it can be applied to the individual Self. As I just said, consciousness has been unfolded by the world, and the LOGOS meticulously planned the world for this unfolding of consciousness. This is why the would-be yogi, picking his objects and following his rules, finds in the world exactly what he needs to make his practice of Yoga real, an important thing that speeds up the knowledge of the Self. There are lots of rules. You have the power to pick and choose which ones you need, avoid the ones you don't, and use the ones you do need. This lets you get the result that nature, without human intelligence, can't do so quickly.

From now on, know that you can do yoga with your own abilities and that even the more basic forms of yoga, like applying the laws of consciousness's development to yourself, will help you in this world and all others. You are really just speeding up your growth and development by using the powers that nature gives you and getting rid of things that are getting in the way of your progress. If you look at it that way, I think Yoga will seem much more real and useful to you than when you just read bits and pieces about it that were taken from Sanskrit books and then translated into English. You will start to realise that being a yogi isn't just something for a life far away, an incarnation that is very different from this one.

Dual Nature of Man

There are some terms used in yoga that you have to know. Because yoga studies people for a specific reason and only cares about two important things about them: their mind and body. To begin, he is a unit, an awareness unit. That is an important point to fully understand. There is only one of him in each set of boxes, and the Theosophist has to change some of his ideas about people before he can start writing this practical line. Theosophy separates people into many parts and pieces, which is a good way to understand how people are put together. We talk about etheric, emotional, physical, and so on. We also talk about Sukshma-sarira, Karana-sarira, Sthula-sarira, and so on. Man is sometimes broken up into Anna-maya-kosa, Prana-maya-kosa, Mano-maya-kosa, and so on. Because we break people up into so many pieces to study them better, it's hard to find the person himself. This is, so to speak, for studying the body and how it works.

But Yoga is both useful and good for you mentally. I'm not upset about the different parts of other schemes. They are necessary for those processes to work. In yoga, on the other hand, a person is only seen as a mind and body, a single awareness contained within a set of envelopes. This is not the Self and the Not-Self being two different things. In yoga, "Self" is awareness plus matter that it can't separate from itself, and "Not-Self" is only the matter that it can leave behind.

Samvid, man is not pure Self or pure awareness. That's not a real thing. In the real world, there is always the Self and His sheaths, even if they aren't very strong. This means that a unit of consciousness can't exist without matter, and a Jivatma, or Monad, is always consciousness plus matter.

So that this is clear, two words are used in Yoga to describe what a man is Prana and Pradhana, air and matter, are life and death. Prana is the air that breathes life into the body. It is also the life force of the universe, or the "life side" of the universe.

He says, "My name is Prana." In this case, "prana" refers to all of life's forces. They are thought to be awareness and mind. The word for matter is pradhana. For a yogi in practice, "body," or "the opposite of mind," means all the taken-over matter from the outside world that he can separate from himself and his own awareness.

This split is very important and useful if you can get the main idea straight. Of course, if you look at it from start to finish, you will see Prana, the great life or self, present in everything, along with the envelopes, bodies, or sheaths that are present at different stages and taking on different forms. But from the point of view of yogic practice, that is Prana, or self, that man identifies with at the moment, along with every sheath of matter that he can't separate himself from in consciousness. For a yogi, that measure is the Self, which means it is a changing amount. As he drops one sheath after another and says, "That is not myself," he gets closer and closer to his greatest point, which is consciousness in a single film, an atom of matter, or a monad. Through the lens of yoga, the active, aware man is so much of himself that he can't separate from the matter that surrounds him or connects him to it. The man can only put his body down and say, "This is not I, but mine." In Yoga, we find that there are a lot of terms that we may use again and again. According to Vyasa, all mental states exist on all planes. This way of understanding people lets us use the same important words over and over again, but with progressively less clear meanings. These meanings become relative and are true at every stage of growth.

Most of us can clearly say, "It is not myself" when it comes to our bodies. This means that when you first start practicing yoga, all the words used to describe the different mental and spiritual states will be relative to the lowest state, which is waking consciousness in the body. You need to carefully look at your own consciousness and figure out how much of it is really consciousness and how much is matter that you can't separate from yourself. Only then can you start to apply the different terms used to describe mental states to yourselves.

Cognitive States

Let us take it in detail. Four states of consciousness are spoken of amongst us. "Waking" consciousness or Jagrat; the "dream" consciousness, or Svapna; the "deep sleep" consciousness, or Sushupti; and the state beyond that, called Turiya. How are those related to the body?

This is the normal waking awareness that you and I are using right now. Our consciousness can work in the subtle, or astral, body and imprint its events on the brain. This is called Svapna, which means "dream consciousness." It is more vivid and real than the Jagrat state. When working in the subtler form—the mental body—it can't imprint its experiences on the brain. This is known as Sushupti or deep sleep awareness, and it means that the mind is working on its own thoughts and not on things in the outside world. But if it has cut itself off from the brain so much that it is hard to remember through outside means, it is called Turiya, which means "high state of trance." When connected to the four planes, these four states show an awareness that has grown a lot. The physical is linked to Jagrat, the spirit is linked to Svapna, the mental is linked to Sushupti, and the Buddhist is linked to Turiya. When we move from one world to another, these words should be used to describe the consciousness that is acting in each world. But the books of Yoga use the same words over and over again, but in different ways. That's where the trouble starts if we haven't learned how they relate to each other. Not everyone has the same Svapna or Sushupti.

The word samadhi is used in many ways and for many reasons, which I will explain in a moment. So how are we supposed to find our way through this mess?

To make sure the process always starts at the same point, you need to know the state. You all know what it means to be awake and aware in the body. You can find four states in that, too, if you look closely. The mind's states follow the same pattern on every plane.

So how do you tell them apart? Let's look at the waking state of mind and try to figure out what the four states are. Let's say I pick up a book and read it. When I read the words, my eyes moved in a way that connected to my outer physical awareness. That's the state of Jagrat. I look past the words to find out what they mean. In the Svapna state of waking awareness, I can see through the outer form and find the inner life. This is different from the waking state of the physical plane. I move on to the writer's mind. This is where the mind touches the mind; this is the waking awareness in the Sushupti state. If I can leave this relationship and live in the writer's mind, I will have reached the Turiya state of waking consciousness.

Use a different example. All I do is look at any watch. I'm in Jagrat. With my eyes closed, I picture the watch. I am in Svapna. I put together a lot of different watch plans and find the perfect one. I am in Sushupti. To the idea of time in a general sense, I pass; I am in Turiya. But these are just stages of my awareness on the physical plane; I haven't left my body yet.

In this way, you can turn mental states into real things that can be understood.

Samadhi

You need to understand some other important words that show up in the Yoga-sutras, even though there aren't exact English translations. Because you have to use them to avoid awkward roundabouts, it's important to describe them. Many people say that "Yoga is Samadhi." In samadhi, the mind is so separate from the body that the body is not aware of what is going on around it. In this trance-like state, the mind is fully aware of itself, but the body is not. The mind then comes back to the body with the experiences it had in the superphysical state and remembers them when it is back in the physical brain. Samadhi is different for each person depending on their level of awareness when they are awake, but it means that their body is not responsive. When a normal person goes into a dream and is on the astral plane, his Samadhi is also there. In the mental plane, where his awareness works, Samadhi is. A person can reach Samadhi if they can separate themselves from their body so much that it doesn't feel anything while their mind is fully aware of themselves.

The saying "Yoga is Samadhi" refers to things that are very important and teach us a lot. Let's say that the only time you can reach the astral world is when you are asleep. In that state, your awareness is in the Svapna state, as we saw. But as you slowly develop your powers, the astral forms start to invade your waking physical awareness. Eventually, they become as clear to you as physical forms, becoming things you are aware of while you are awake. The astral world is now part of your Jagrat consciousness instead of your Svapna consciousness. You now have the physical world and the astral world as parts of your Jagrat consciousness. The thought world is still part of your Svapna consciousness. Then "your body" includes both the real body and the astral body. As you go on, the mental plane starts to come in too, and the physical, astral, and mental all become a part of your waking awareness. This is your Jagrat world. These three worlds are like one world to you, and their three bodies are like one body that sees and acts. If you are a yogi, your three bodies have become one body. When things are like this, you can only see one world at a time if you put your attention on it. It is possible to focus on the physical and see it when you are in that state of expanded waking. The astral and mental will then look fuzzy. Putting your mind on the astral will help you see it. The mental and physical will then look fuzzy and dim. Remember that I can focus my eyes in this hall on the middle of the hall, making the pillars on either side look fuzzy. This will make sense to you. Or, I might focus on a structure and clearly see it, but I might not be able to make out you at the same time. It's not a change of body, but a change of mind. Remember that the yogi's body is everything that can be thrown away as not being themselves. As you rise, the lower bodies merge into one body, and the awareness inside the sheath of matter that it still can't throw away becomes the man.

He said, "Yoga is Samadhi." It gives you the power to focus on yourself and pull away from everything you know as body. We call that Samadhi. After that, no normal way will be able to bring you back to the world you left. This also explains the part of The Secret Doctrine that says the Adept "begins his Samadhi on the atmic plane." A Jivan-mukta starts his journey into Samadhi on the atmic plane. For him, all the planes below the atmic are the same. As a man, he can't reach the level of Samadhi he starts on. He starts on the atmic plane and moves up to the higher cosmic planes one step at a time. One word, samadhi, is used to describe different states of consciousness. In a normal person's self-induced trance, the consciousness rises above the physical into the astral. In a Jivan-mukta, the consciousness rises to the higher planes of a larger world, even though it is already centred in the fifth, or atmic, plane.

Yogic Literature

People who don't know Sanskrit will be disappointed to learn that most Yoga material is not available in English. The Upanishads and the Bhagavad-Gita are where you can find the general lessons of Yoga. You can easily find these texts in many translations, but they are only general; they give you the main ideas but not specifics about how to do them. You are told to make sacrifices, lose interest in things, and so on, but the Bhagavad-Gita only tells you that these things are moral rules that you must follow. It doesn't tell you how to reach the goals it sets. Some of the most important books in yoga are the smaller Upanishads, also known as "the hundred and eight." Then there is the Tantras, which are a huge body of writing. The average English person thinks that these books are bad, but they're not quite right. The Tantras are very valuable and helpful books that teach you everything you need to know about the magic. But they can be broken down into three groups: those who work with white magic, those who work with black magic, and those who work with "grey magic," which is a mix of the two. Now, the word "magic" refers to the planned ways of causing physical states that are not normal by using your will.

When nerves are tense because of stress or illness, it can lead to normal hysteria, which is both emotional and stupid. The will also creates a similar high level of stress that makes a person sensitive to vibrations outside of matter. Going to sleep doesn't mean anything, but entering Samadhi is a powerful state that can't be bought. The process is mostly the same, but one is caused by normal circumstances and the other by the skilled will at work. The Yogi is someone who has learned about the power of will and how to use it to get results that were already planned. That which we know has always been called magic. It is the name of the Great Science of the past, the one Science that was only called "great" in the past. The Tantras have everything in them: the magical side of both people and nature, the ways to make discoveries, and the rules for how people can make new versions of themselves. The problem is that they are very dangerous to use without a teacher. Many times, a man who tries to use

Tantric methods without a teacher gets very sick. In the West and here in India, the Tantras have a bad name. A lot of the "occult" books sold in the United States today are just translated bits and pieces of the Tantras. The fact that these Tantric works often use the name of a body part to stand for a spirit or mental centre is a problem. There is some truth to that because all the centres are linked from body to body, but a good teacher wouldn't let their student work on the body's parts until the student had some control over the higher centres and the body was clean. When you know one, you can better understand the other, and a teacher who has been through it all can lead his student in the right direction. But if you pick up these physical words without knowing what they mean, you will get lost and might even hurt yourself. There is a Sutra that says if you focus on a certain part of your tongue, you will be able to see the spirit world. So, if you focus your attention on the pituitary body, just above this part of the tongue, you will be able to see the spirit world. The word for a centre has a physical counterpart, and the word is often used to refer to the body's parts when it should be used for a centre. This is called a "blind," and it's meant to keep people from doing dangerous things that are written about in books. People can meditate on that part of their tongues for the rest of their lives and nothing bad will happen, but if they think on the corresponding centre in their body, a lot of bad things may happen. "Think about your navel," it's also said. There is a close link between this and the solar plexus, so it must mean that. If you think about that too much, though, you could get a major mental illness that is hard to recover from. Those who know how many people in India suffer because of these practices are aware that it is not a good idea to jump into them without first getting some advice on what they mean and what is safe to do and what is not. The sutras of Patanjali are the other part of the Yoga texts. That is out there, but I fear that not many people will be able to make much of it on their own. In the first place, there is a lot of commentary in Sanskrit that is only partly translated into English that explains the Sutras, which are just headings. Even the comments are strange in that they only repeat the hardest words without explaining them, which doesn't help the student learn much.

Diverse Connotations

Some words that keep coming up need short explanations so that no one gets confused. These words are: unfolding, evolution, spirituality, psychism, yoga, and mysticism.

While "evolution" always refers to forms, "unfolding" always refers to consciousness. What is homogeneous turns into heterogeneous, and what is simple turns into complicated. Still, Spirit and awareness don't grow or get better; they are already there and never will be. The only thing that can happen to them is that they will turn outward instead of staying inward. The God inside of you can't change, but He can show off His power through matter that He has taken over for the purpose, and the matter changes to serve Him.

What He is all that He shows. And this may make you think of many sayings by great mystics: “Become,” says St. Ambrose, “what you are”; this is a strange phrase, but it says a lot: become in the outside world what you are in the inside. That is what the whole process of yoga is meant to do.

Seeing the One is what “spirituality” means. “Psychism” is the idea that mind can show up in any material form.

As a science, “yoga” is the search for union through the mind. As a feeling, “mysticism” is the search for the same union through the heart. That’s right, the word “yoga” can be used to describe any way of becoming one with oneself. I’m using it in a broader sense here, as something that has to do with intelligence and is called a science, following Patanjali.

Look at the mystic. When he focuses on the object of his devotion, he forgets about himself and falls into a rapture of love and adoration. He forgets about everything else and is swept up to God by a great wave of feeling. He has no idea how he got to that high level. He is only aware of God and how much he loves Him. The mystic’s bliss and the saint’s victory are here.

That’s not how the yogi works. He starts to understand what he is doing step by step. Science, not feeling, guides his work. This means that people who don’t like science because they find it dull and dry aren't developing the part of themselves that will benefit most from Yoga right now. The yogi could use dedication as a way to do this. This is made very clear in Patanjali. There are many ways to follow Yoga, and it's interesting that "devotion to Isvara" is one of them. The spirit of the scientific thought comes out. For him, devotion to Isvara is not an end in itself. Instead, it is a way to reach his main goal, which is to focus his mind. Right away, you can see the change in spirit. It is the way of the mystic to be devoted to Isvara. That's how he comes to know togetherness. If you look at devotion to Isvara from a scientific point of view, it's a way to focus your thoughts. This is the best way to explain the spiritual difference between Yoga and Mysticism. This person sees loyalty to Isvara as a way to reach the Beloved, while the other person sees it as a way to focus. For a mystic, God is the thing they are looking for; they want to be one with Him in consciousness; and they are delighted in Him. For a yogi, on the other hand, focusing on God is just a good way to clear their thoughts. To get to one goal, loyalty is used. To get to the other goal, God is seen as the goal and is reached directly through rapture.

God Outside and God Within

That brings us to the next point: how God outside and God inside are related. The yogi, who is a type of Hindu thought, says that the only sure proof of God is the witness of the Self within that He exists. The yogi's idea for finding proof of God is to remove all limitations from your consciousness until you have pure consciousness with only a thin veil of nirvanic matter covering it. After that, you'll know that God is. In the Upanishad, it says, "Whose only proof is the witness of the Self." From the way people think in the West, who try to prove God through arguments, this is very different. A Hindu will tell you that you can't show that God exists through any kind of argument or reasoning. He says that God is beyond reason, so even if reason helps you along the way, it won't prove that God exists. You can only get to know Him by going deep inside yourself. In that place, you will find Him and know that He is both inside and outside of you. Yoga is a way to clear your mind of everything that isn't God, except for the veil of the nirvanic atom, which lets you know for sure that God exists. For Hindus, the only thing that can be called faith is an inner belief. This is why faith is said to be beyond reason and is often mistaken for believability. Faith goes beyond reason because it's the Self's testimony to himself—that conviction of existing as Self, of which reason is just one of the outward manifestations. And the only real faith is that inner conviction of the Self within you, which no argument can strengthen or weaken, and which you are completely sure of. Yoga is meant to help you reach that Self all the time, not just by having a sudden intuitive insight, but slowly, unwaveringly, and consistently. Once you reach that Self, the question "Is there a God?" will never come up again.

Evolutions in Awareness and Material Resonances

It is important to know something about the consciousness that is your Self and the matter that is the envelope of awareness but that the Self often confuses for itself. The most important thing about awareness is that it changes, and you can be sure that it does. Life's awareness doesn't change, but everything else does. It is only through changes that consciousness becomes Self-consciousness. Being conscious is something that changes all the time, but there is one idea that doesn't change: self-existence. No matter where or how you are, your awareness doesn't change. It only changes how it feels inside itself.

Every change in matter starts with a shift in where it is. Things change when their states change, and states change when things change places. Also, every change in awareness is linked to vibrations in the matter that it travels in. When we look closely at matter, we find three basic qualities: sattva, rajas, and tamas. These are rhythm, movement, and stability. Sattva is movement and music. Rasa, or movement, is not all it is. It is a controlled movement, a swinging from side to side over a set distance. It is also called a wave length or vibration.

People often ask, "How can things that belong to such different groups, like matter and Spirit, affect each other?" "Can we cross that huge gap that some say can never be filled?" The Indian has crossed it, or rather, he has shown that there isn't a split. For the Indian, matter and spirit are not only two sides of the same thing, but by looking closely at the connection between consciousness and matter, he can see that in every universe, the LOGOS forces matter to follow a specific set of rhythms, with each vibration of matter corresponding to a shift in consciousness. No change in consciousness, no matter how small, has not been linked to a vibration in matter, and no vibration in matter, no matter how fast or delicate, has not been linked to a certain change in consciousness. To build the atom, the Hindu scriptures talk about the Tanmatra, which means "the measure of That" or "the measure of consciousness." This is the first great work of the LOGOS. There are an endless number of vibrations that the consciousness that is him forces on his material every time consciousness changes. So there is always this link between the Self and his sheaths: changes in awareness cause changes in the vibration of matter, and vice versa. That lets the Self understand the Not-Self.

Ratha Yoga, Hatha Yoga, the Kingly Yoga, and the Yoga of Resolve all use these correspondences. The goal of Raja Yoga is to control the changes in awareness so that you can also control the things that you're made of. In Hatha Yoga, the goal is to change the way people think and feel by controlling the energy of matter. Another problem with Hatha Yoga is that its actions can only affect the astral plane. Also, the heavy stress put on the physically-based matter can cause organs to shrink, even though they need to be active in order to bring about the desired changes in consciousness. The Hatha Yogi takes charge of the parts of the body that the waking awareness no longer cares about because it has given them over to the "subconsciousness." This is often helpful for keeping people from getting sick, but it doesn't serve any higher purpose. He is in a dangerous area of the brain when he works on the parts that control regular consciousness and even more so when he touches the parts that control super-consciousness. He is more likely to become paralysed than to evolve.

The only thing that makes matter cognizable is that relationship. When the mind changes, something changes outside of him, and when he changes something, it changes outside of him. answer: rearrange the body's matter again; it's his envelope. Because of this, the way matter changes in a regular way is called its cognizability. Matter can be known by awareness because the relationship between the two sides of the manifest LOGOS, which is one, doesn't change. The Self is aware of changes within himself and, by extension, of changes in the words around him.

Mind

What is the mind? In the yogic view, mind is just the individual consciousness, which means the whole of your consciousness, including your actions. In Western psychology, mind is separate from consciousness.

Yoga is only possible if you understand Eastern thinking. What words can we use to explain this unique consciousness? To begin, it knows things. It wants them now that it knows about them. It tries to get them because it wants them. There are three parts of consciousness: knowledge, desire, and action. On the physical plane, there is a lot of action, but there is also desire and thought. Wishes rule the spirit plane, and they can change what you think and do. When it comes to the mind, intelligence is the main note, and action and desire are affected by it. When you go to the Buddhist plane, pure reason, or thought, rules, and so on. There is always one of each trait, but one stands out more. The same goes for the things that belong to them. Your combinations of matter give you rhythmic, active, or stable ones. The conditions of the activity of all of these in your awareness will depend on the combinations of matter in your bodies. To do yoga, you have to build your body around the rhythmic patterns that make action and inertia less clear. The yogi wants his body to match his mind.

Stages of Mind

PāĹā says that the mind has five stages, and Vyasa says that "these stages of mind are on every plane." The mind is thrown around in the first stage, called the Kshipta stage. This is the butterfly mind, the early stage of humanity, or the mind of a child in humans, which is always moving from one thing to another. It's the same as doing something on the real plane.

The next stage is the confused stage, Mudha, which is like the stage of a young person who is swayed and confused by their feelings. He starts to feel like he doesn't know anything, which is a state that goes beyond the changeableness of a child and is typical of activity in the astral world. The next state is Vikshipta, which means "preoccupation" or "infatuation." This is the state of a person who is driven by an idea, like love, desire, or something else. No longer is he a young man who doesn't know what he wants, but a man who does and has an idea. It could be the set idea that drives a crazy person or the idea that makes a hero or saint; either way, the idea owns him. The difference between a maniac and a martyr is the idea itself—whether it is true or wrong.

He is stuck on a single idea, which makes him either crazy or a hero. There is no reason to argue against it. If he has already told himself that he is made of glass, no amount of reasoning will change his mind. His view of himself will always be that he is as fragile as glass. That is a fixed thought that isn't true. But there is one idea that defines a hero and a victim. Everything must be thrown away for a great truth that is more important than life. That thing has taken over his life, and he is willing to die for it. That kind of state is said to be close to Yoga because the person is becoming focused, even if they are only focused on one thought. The lower mental plane is where this step takes place. The fourth stage is when a person owns a thought instead of being controlled by it. This single-pointed state of mind is called Ekagrata in Sanskrit. He's grown up and ready for real life. When a person has lived their whole life based on a single idea, they are getting closer to yoga. They are free from the world's pull and are no longer affected by its temptations. When he has what he used to have, though, he is ready for Yoga and can start the training that helps him make quick progress. The activity at this time is on the higher mental plane.

This fourth stage, called Ekagrata, leads to the fifth stage, called Niruddha, which means "self-controlled." People are self-controlled and can do yoga well when they don't just have one idea, but rise above all of them and choose what they want, taking or not taking according to their illumined will. This stage is like what happens on the Buddhist plane.

In the third stage, Vikshipta, he is controlled by the idea and learning Viveka, which means telling the difference between what is real and what is not real. After learning the lesson of Viveka, he moves on to the next level, Ekagrata. In this level, he picks one idea, like the inner life, and keeps his mind on it. As he does this, he learns Vairagya, or lack of emotion. He rises above the need to own things that make him happy, whether they are from this world or another. Then he moves on to the fifth step, which is self-control. The Shatsamapatti, or six blessings, are what he needs to do to get there. These six gifts deal with the Will part of consciousness. Viveka and Vairagya, on the other hand, deal with the Thinking and Doing parts.

You can tell how ready you are to start the serious practice of Yoga by studying your own mind. Look into your thought to see if you can spot these stages in yourself. You are not ready for Yoga if you are in either of the first two stages. The young person, the child, and the busy man are not ready to become yogis. But if you feel like you are taken over by a single thought, you are almost ready for yoga. This is the next step of one-pointedness, where you can pick your idea and stick to it by your own will. Short is the path from there to full control, which can stop the thought from moving at all. After getting to that point, going into Samadhi is pretty easy.

Inner and Outer Awareness

Sati has two forms: one that faces outward and one that faces inward. Being aware of the outside world is always first. In this stage of Samadhi, your awareness has turned outward. This is when you can go beyond the things that they represent and see the principles that they are made of. This is when you catch a glimpse of life through their form. At this point, Darwin got a glimpse of the truth about evolution. That is the Samadhi of the body that faces outward.

Though this is called Samprajnata Samadhi, which means "Samadhi with consciousness," I think it's better to think of it as having consciousness turned outward, meaning aware of things around you. It is called "Samadhi without consciousness" because it happens when the object goes away, or when awareness separates from the sheath through which objects are seen. I like the term "inward-turned consciousness" better because this stage is reached by turning away from the outside world.

In every way, these two stages of Samadhi happen one after the other. In the first stage, you focus very hard on objects, which pierces through the outer form to the underlying principle. The next stage is when your consciousness turns away from the sheath that served its purpose and pulls inward, into a sheath that you don't yet recognise as a sheath. Then, for a while, it is only aware of itself and not the outside world. Then there is the "cloud," which is the beginning of a dim feeling of "something" outside of itself. This is followed by the functioning of the nigher sheath and the recognition of the objects on the next higher plane, which corresponds to the sheath. The full circle goes like this: Samprajnata Samadhi, Asamprajnata Samadhi, Megha (cloud), Samprajnata Samadhi of the next plane, and so on.

The Cloud

The commentators don't say much about this word, which is Dharma-megha, which means "cloud of righteousness" or "cloud of religion." In fact, the only thing they can say is that the man's good karma from the past comes together and rains down joy on him.

We should try to find something more than this weak explanation.

In Western mystic writing, the word "cloud" is used a lot. For example, the student knows of the "Cloud on the Mount," the "Cloud on the Sanctuary," and the "Cloud on the Mercy-Seat." And the experience they talk about is something that all mystics have had in its lower stages and for some, it's been in its fullness. In its early stages, it is this experience where the awareness withdraws into a sheath that isn't yet recognised as a sheath. This is followed by the beginning of that sheath's functioning, which is shown by a faint sense of an outer. You feel like you're surrounded by thick fog. You know you're not alone, but you can't see. Hold your breath, be calm, and wait. Make sure your mind is in a state of tension. Soon, the cloud will start to thin, and you'll catch views of a higher plane, and then it will dawn on you in all its glory. This entrance into a higher plane will happen over and over again until your consciousness is no longer focused on the buddhic plane and its beauty has faded. As your consciousness pulls back from that beautiful sheath, you find yourself in the true cloud, the cloud over the sanctuary, the cloud that covers the Holiest, and the cloud that hides the vision of the Self. Then what seems like the life literally drains away, the last hold on the real is lost, and there is nothing but horror, loneliness that can't be described. Hold out, endure. Everything needs to go. "Nothing outside of the Eternal can help you." Scripture says, "Be still, and know that I am God."

This means that God can only be seen when there is silence. A voice, the voice of the self, will be heard in that silence. There will be a life, the life of the Self, felt in that silence. In that empty space, the fullness of the self will be shown. There will be a Light, the glory of the Self, in that darkness. The cloud will go away, and the Self's shining will become clear. What was just a glimpse of a faraway glory will become a permanent reality, and when you know the Self and how you are one with it, you will enter the Peace that only the Self has.

Chapter 2
Intellectual Traditions of Yoga

Anyone who knows the language Sanskrit and is interested in psychology should know how useful it is for talking about the subject in an exact and scientific way. The Sanskrit language, which means "well-made," "constructed," or "built-together," is the best for explaining mental problems. The shape of a word is used over and over to give hints, explain things, or show connections. As a result of the way the language is built, a single word can have many meanings. This means that when you speak or use Sanskrit, you can use this word link to find all related ideas, truths, or facts. Very few of its roots are important, but it has a huge number of words built on those bases.

YUJ is the root of the word yoga, which comes from a word that means "to join." This root is found in many languages, including English, where it comes from the Latin word jugare, jungere, which also means "to join." Many English words come from this root, such as junction, conjunction, disjunction, and so on. Again, the English word "yoke" comes from the same Sanskrit root. By looking at the different words, ideas, or facts that are linked to this root, you can figure out what the word "yoga" means and how broad it is in its application to everyday mental processes. Many of the words that are linked to it are also very suggestive, leading you to the meaning. Like in French, English speakers constantly use a word similar to rapport: "being en rapport," which is a French phrase that has been Anglicised so much that we hear it all the time. In some ways, that word is the most like the Sanskrit word yoga, which means "to be connected with," "to enter into," "to merge in," and other similar words. All of these meanings are grouped together under the word "Yoga." Sri Krishna saying "Yoga is equilibrium" in Sanskrit means exactly what it sounds like: balance. Yoga means yoking, and the Sanskrit word for equilibrium is "samvata," which means "togetherness." This is a very simple, direct statement that doesn't mean anything deep; it's just expressing one of the basic meanings of the word He's using. So, here's another word from the comments on the Sutra that has a very clear meaning for Hindus: "Yoga is Samadhi." For someone who only knows English, that doesn't really say anything; each word needs to be explained. A man who knows Sanskrit would know that the two words go together. As we saw, the word yoga means "joined together," and the word samadhi comes from the root dha, which means "to place," along with the words sam and a, which mean "completely together." So, Samadhi basically means "putting everything together," and its English translation would be "to compose" (com = sam; posita = place). So, samadhi means "composing the mind," or getting the mind together and rid of all the things that are distracting it. Thus, both a linguistic and a practical study of the language shows that the words yoga and samadhi are inextricably linked. When the commentator Vyasa says, "Yoga is the composed mind," he is making a clear and important point about what Yoga means. By natural progression of ideas, Samadhi has come to mean the trance-like state that comes from being completely calm. However, its original meaning should not be forgotten.

When trying to explain Yoga, it can be hard to find the right English words to match the many meanings of the Sanskrit language. I strongly suggest that those of you who can learn this beautiful language do so. This will help you understand the literature of Yoga better than someone who doesn't know any Sanskrit at all.

Indian Philosophies

Please take a moment to think about how Yoga fits in with two of the most important schools of Hindu philosophy. Without understanding the basics of these great schools of philosophy, neither people from the West nor people from India who don't know Sanskrit can fully appreciate the translations of the most important Indian books that are popular now in the West and the power of all the references they make. Pick up the Bhagavad-Gita. There are probably a lot of people who know that book pretty well and use it to help them with their spiritual life but don't know most of what it says. Although reading it, you will always be somewhat in the dark unless you know that it is based on an Indian philosophy called the Samkhya and that the meaning of almost all the technical words in it is limited by what they mean in that philosophy.

There are some phrases that are more Vedanta-like, but the vast majority are Samkhyan. It is assumed that anyone reading or using the book knows what Samkhyan thought is all about. While I don't want to go into specifics, I need to give you a sense of the philosophy's main ideas. If you understand these, you will not only be able to read the Bhagavad-Gita much more intelligently, but you will also be able to use it for yogic reasons in a way that is almost impossible if you don't know these things.

The words used in the Bhagavad-Gita and the Yoga-sutras of Patanjali are both Samkhyan. Yoga's philosophy is built on the Samkhya, which is important to remember. Samkhya doesn't care about the existence of God; it only cares about how the world comes to be, or the order of evolution. Because of this, it is sometimes called Nir-isvara Samkhya, which means "Samkhya without God." However, it is linked to the Yoga system so deeply that the Yoga system is known as Sesvara Samkhya, which means "with God." To help you understand it, let me describe a part of the Samkhya philosophy that talks about the relationship between Spirit and matter. Notice how this differs from the Vedantic view of Self and Not-Self, and then find how the Theosophical view of nature's facts makes sense. You might think that the Lord of Yoga's instructions in the Gita are sometimes at odds with each other because they are written in both Samkhyan and Vedantic language. These languages come from different points of view, one seeing the world through the lens of matter and the other through the lens of Spirit. If you are interested in Theosophy, you will be able to understand the different phrases if you know the facts. That understanding and reconciliation of these words that seem to go against each other is what I want to talk about now.

The first thing that the Samkhyan School says is that the universe is made up of two things: Spirit and Matter, or more correctly, Spirits and Matter. The Spirit is called Purusha, which means "man," and each Spirit is unique. Purusha is a unit, a unit of awareness. They are all the same thing, but they will always be different from each other. There are a lot of these groups; there are a lot of Purushas in the world of men. But even though there are a huge number of them, they are all the same; they are uniform. Each Purusha has three traits that are the same between them all. One trait is awareness, which will soon turn into intellect. Living things, or prana, are the second trait; it will become movement. The third trait is immutability, which is what infinity is all about; it will become will. Some people think that eternity means time that never ends, but it's not. Eternity and time that never ends are not the same thing. Eternity and time are not the same thing at all. Eternity is changeless, unchanging, and all at the same time. Even if time went on forever, that wouldn't be enough to give infinity. The fact that Purusha can't change shows that He is eternal, since something that doesn't change is something that is eternal.

The Samkhya says that these are the three qualities of Purusha. The names for these are different from the Vedantic Sat, Chit, and Ananda, but they are very much the same. Being aware or knowing is Chit; life or force is Sat; and immutability, which is what infinity is all about, is Ananda.

The second part of the Samkhyan split is Prakriti, which means matter. It stands in contrast to the Purushas, which are uniform units that number in the millions. There is only one Prakriti, but many Purushas. While Prakriti is a continuum, Purushas are discontinuous because they are made up of many identical parts. With Prakriti, things stay the same. Take a moment to think about the name Prakriti. Let's look into what it means at its core. The name tells you what it is. The word "make" comes from the root "pra," which means "forth." In this way, Prakriti means "forth-making matter is that which makes the essence of being become." That which is Being (is-tence) turns into ex-is-tence (outbeing) through Matter. To say that Matter "makes forth" is to say what it is all about in a single word. Spirit, also known as Purusha, can only "make" himself through Prakriti. If Prakriti isn't there, Purusha is powerless and just an idea. Being in and with Prakriti is the only way for Purusha to use his skills. Prakriti also has three qualities, or gunas, which are well-known terms for traits or features. These are speed, movement, and stillness. Rhythm makes it possible for awareness to turn into thought. Being able to move around makes life active. It is inertia that makes immutability into will.

Now, the idea of how Spirit and Matter are connected is a very strange one, and many false beliefs come from having mixed ideas about it. Understanding this makes the Bhagavad-Gita clearer, and it's easy to see how the words about action and actor, as well as the mistake of saying "I act," refer to technical Samkhyan ideas.

When Prakriti is separated from Purusha, its three traits are balanced, still, and stacked against each other, cancelling each other out. This is why Matter is called jada, which means "unconscious" or "dead." But everything changes when Purusha is around. When Purusha is close to Matter, Matter changes, not from the outside but from the inside.

Vyasa says that Purusha works on Prakriti by proximity. When it gets close to Prakriti, Prakriti starts to live. The "coming near" is a figure of speech that fits our ideas of time and space, since we can't say that Spirit is "near." Spirit is timeless and exists in no place. The word "propinquity" refers to the effect that Purusha has on Prakriti. In the case of material things, this effect is caused by their closeness to each other. Putting a magnet close to a soft iron piece or an electric body close to a neutral body will change the soft iron or the neutral body in some ways. The soft iron is a magnet because it is close to a magnet; it has the properties of a magnet, like having poles that show up, attracting steel, and either pulling or pushing the end of an electric needle. When there is a positively charged body nearby, the electricity in a neutral body is rearranged so that the positively charged body moves away and the negatively charged body gathers close to the positively charged body. Both times, an internal change happened because of how close one item was to the other. The same goes for Purusha and Prakriti. Purusha doesn't do anything, but it has an effect on the world, like a magnetic field. When Purusha acts on the three gunas, they go through a wonderful change. I'm not sure what words to use so I don't mess it up. You can't say that Prakriti takes in the effect. It's not really true that it shows the Purusha. The appearance of Purusha, on the other hand, changes things inside Prakriti and throws off the balance of the three gunas. It looked like all three gunas were equal. There was no guna. Another guna was used to balance the first one. What takes place when Purusha affects Prakriti? In Purusha, the quality of awareness is mirrored in the guna called Sattva, which is rhythm. In Prakriti, this quality turns into cognition. In Purusha, the quality we call life is reflected in the guna called Rajas, which means movement. In Prakriti, this quality is turned into force, energy, and action. Innateness is a quality of Purusha that is mirrored in the guna Tamas. Will or desire is a quality of Prakriti that is reflected in Purusha. That is why, in that balanced balance of Prakriti, something has changed just by the Purusha being nearby. The Purusha hasn't lost anything, but things have changed. It now has cognition in it. It now has activity and force in it. There is now will or desire in it. This change in Prakriti leads to another change. If you take the three parts of Purusha away from each other, you can't take the three parts of Prakriti away from each other either. So, while rhythm takes on awareness, it is also affected by the three-in-one Purusha and can't help but also take on life and immutability as action and will. The same goes for movement and stillness. Different qualities can play a big role in different combinations. For example, awareness and rhythm may play a big role in some combinations, while immutability and inertia may play a big role in others. The states where awareness-rhythm or thought rules become "mind in nature," also known as the subject or subjective half of nature. The objective half of nature, or "force and matter" to western scientists, is made up of combinations of the other two.

So, nature is now split in two: the subject and the object. There is now everything in nature that we need for activity to show up, forms to be made, and awareness to be expressed. We have mind, force, and matter. Purusha has nothing else to do because he has put all of his skills into Prakriti. He now just sits there and thinks about how they work together, without changing himself. Things that Matter does are what life is all about; Spirit only looks at it. Purusha is the audience that the play is meant for. Not him, but someone who is just watching. The player is the mind, which is the subjective part of nature and the copy of awareness in rhythmic matter. Objective nature is what makes it work. It shows the other traits of Purusha, like life and immutability, in the gunas, rajas, and tamas. Since nature has everything needed to make the world, it must have worked. The Putusha will only watch a play when it is running in front of him. He's not acting; he's just watching. This is the main idea of the Bhagavad-Gita. Everything is done by nature. The gunas make the world possible. The person who says, "I act," is wrong and confused. It is the gunas who act, not him. His only role is to watch and not do anything. There is a lot of teaching in the Gita that is based on this idea of the Samkhya, and we can't understand what different philosophical words mean until we understand this.

Now let's talk about the idea in the Vedas. The Vedantic view says that the Self is one, everywhere, everything, and the only truth. Vedanta starts with the idea that there is nothing but the Self. There is the Self everywhere, all permeating, all ruling, and all inspiring. The One Self permeates, holds back, supports, and brings life to everything, just like the air permeates all matter. The Gita says that just like air goes everywhere, so does the Self in all the different kinds of things. Follow the outline of Vedantic thought and try to understand the idea of the one universal Self, which is existence, awareness, bliss, and Sat-Chit-Ananda. This leads us to a higher level of philosophy than the Samkhya. There is only one Self. There is consciousness, existence, and happiness in every place where the Self is. These aspects of the Self are not separate from each other. Being everywhere and including everything, these traits can be found everywhere. And you can't point to a place and say, "The Self is not here." The Self is everywhere, and where He is, there is life, awareness, and happiness. As awareness, the Self imagines limits and separation. That idea of limits gives rise to form, variety, and manyness. Everything different about the many comes from that thought of the Self and of limits. Matter is the Self's restraint that He puts on Himself because He wants to. "Eko'ham, bahu syam," which means "I am one; I will be many" or "let me be many," is the Godhead's thought. It is this thought that the infinite world comes into being. He exists, is aware, and is happy in that restriction that He made for Himself. The thought that He is Self-existence comes up in Him, and look! Everything becomes possible. All manifestations happen at the same time because the will to appear is in Him. Because all happiness is in Him, the rule of life is to seek happiness, which is something that all living things must do. The world shows up when you limit your thoughts on yourself. Because the world is not what the Self thinks it is, it goes away like a dream. That is what the Vedanta is all about. Then it lets the Samkhya gods come in.

The Purushas, but it says that these spirits are really just reflections of the one Self, sent out by the activity of the Self, and that they are all tiny versions of Him, limited by the limitations that the universal Self put on them. They look like parts of the universe, but they are really the same as Him. The Supreme Self's play creates limitations, which then reproduces the qualities of the Self. The Supreme Self's consciousness becomes cognition, or the power to know; the particularised Self's existence becomes activity, or the power to make things happen; and the particularised Self's bliss becomes will, or the deepest desire for happiness and bliss. The resolve to achieve it is what we call will. So, the limited has the power to know, the power to act, and the power to will. These are the qualities of the particular Self that mirror the qualities of the universal Self. In other words, what was universal awareness is now cognition in the divided Self; what was awareness of itself in the universal Self is now awareness of others in the limited Self; and what was awareness of the whole becomes cognition of the individual. In the same way, the existence of the Self changes the Self-existence of the universal Self into action and the preservation of existence in the limited Self. But the happiness of the universal Self becomes the will to be happy in the restricted form of the individual Self. This is the Self-determination of the Self, the seeking for Self-realization, which is at the heart of all human life.

The difference comes from being limited, from turning the qualities that are true for everyone into the qualities of the limited Self. They are the same in core, but they show up differently. We are able to know, will, and do things. These are the three main powers of the Self. They show up in the split Self in a huge range of shapes and sizes, from the smallest cell to the biggest Logos.

In the same way that in Samkhya there is delusion and bondage when the Purusha, or specific Self, identifies with the matter in which he is reflected, so there is delusion and bondage when the Self, who is eternally free, identifies with matter and his limitations, he is in the domain of Maya. This is because Maya is when the Self identifies with his limitations. Matter can never bind the eternally free, the eternally pure, the eternally aware, or the eternally Self-determined. Matter can only rule the eternally ignorant. His own stupid imagination limits his natural abilities. He is limited because he thinks he is limited; he is dirty because he thinks he is dirty; he doesn't know anything because he thinks he doesn't know anything. When his fantasy goes away, he realises that he is always pure and wise.

This is the main difference between Vedanta and Samkhya. The Samkhya says that Purusha is always an observer and never an actor. The Vedanta theory says that the Self is the only actor and that everything else is maya. It says that there is no one else who acts but the Self. The Upanishad says that when the Self wanted to see, eyes and ears appeared. When the Self wanted to think, thought appeared. The eyes, ears, and mind are all real because the Self willed them to be. Matter is taken over by the Self so that He can show off His skills through it. There is a difference between the Samkhya and the Vedanta. In the Samkhya, the closeness of the Purusha brings out all of these qualities in matter or Prakriti, but it is Prakriti that acts, not the Purusha. In the Vedanta, on the other hand, the Self exists and acts by itself; He imagines limitation and matter appears, and He takes that matter to show His own power.

Those who are scientists see the world through the lens of Samkhya, while those who are metaphysicians see it through the lens of Vedanta. Without meaning to, Haeckel explained the Samkhyan philosophy almost correctly. Because his explanation is so close to the

Samkhyan, another idea would make it completely Samkhyan. He hasn't yet added the proximity of consciousness that the Samkhya assumes in its final duality. He has Mind in Matter and Force, but not Purusha. Sir Oliver Lodge didn't like his last book, but from a Hindu point of view, it makes perfect sense and is a very good reflection of Samkhyan thought. This is the scientist's point of view, who doesn't care about the "why" of the facts he writes down. As I already said, the metaphysician's view is Vedanta. He looks for the unity that all differences come from and that solves them.

Now, what does Theosophy say about these two ideas? Theosophy helps all thinkers make sense of words that seem to be so clearly at odds with each other. Theosophy and Vedanta both talk about the universal Self. It says the same things about the general Self and the Self-limitation that Vedanta does. We call these restricted selves Monads, and like the Vedantin, we say that they have the same nature as the universal Self that they are parts of. So, you can see in them the three things that you see in the Supreme. They are units, and these are the Purushas of the Samkhya. But there is a big difference: they are not passive observers; they are active participants in the story of the universe. Although, since they are above the fivefold universe, they are like spectators who control the actors on the stage. The Monad takes atoms from the world of matter that have the same qualities as his three qualities. He thinks, wills, and acts through these atoms. He comes up with his own musical patterns and shows how smart he is. He uses mobile combos to show what he's up to. He uses the things that don't do anything to show off his happiness, which is the will to be happy. Now look at how phrase and thought are different. Matter changed in the Samkhya to represent the Spirit. In fact, the Spirit takes parts of Matter and uses them to show his own traits, which is a huge difference. He makes an actor for Self-expression. This actor is the "spiritual man" of the Theosophical theory, also known as the spiritual trinity (Atma, Buddha, and Manas), which we will talk about again in a moment.

The Monad is always outside of the fivefold world, so it can be thought of as a spectator. Outside of the five planes of matter, he lives. The planes of Vayu, Agni, Kubera, Varuna, the mind, and the body are all beyond the Atmic, also known as Akasic. The Monad, or Self, stands above all of these worlds. It is self-aware and self-determined. He rules over peace that never changes and lives forever. But, as was already said, he takes things. He takes a tiny piece of the Atmic plane and, in a way, inserts his will into it. This thing then becomes Atma. He takes an atom from the Buddha-plane and thinks about his way of knowing in it. This part of his mind becomes buddhi. In a way, he takes an atom from the manasic plane and puts his action into it, making it Manas. In this way, we get Atma plus Buddhi plus Manas. That triad is the Monad's mirror in the fivefold universe, which is outside of the fivefold universe. It is easy to tell the difference between Theosophy's words and those of other schools. In Theosophy, the Monad is like the Jivatma in Indian thought. It is the Purusha of the Samkhya and the specific Self of Vedanta. The three-fold appearance,

According to Vedantic teaching, Atma-buddhi-manas is what happens when the Purusha is close to Prakriti. Prakriti is the subject of Samkhyan thought and is the Self in the highest sheaths. The Self and His coverings are in one, and the Subject, which is a mirror of Purusha in matter, is in the other. At this point, it's clear that you're talking about the same ideas, but from different points of view. Though we are more connected to Vedanta than to Samkhya, if you know the basic ideas behind both, you can easily separate their claims and not get lost. Before you can explain any theory, you need to know how it works. The benefit of the Theosophical teaching is that it gives you the rules and lets you study the philosophies on your own. You study them with a torch instead of in the dark.

Now that we know what the spiritual man, or Triad, is made of, what do we learn about all the different ways that awareness shows itself? That they are two souls, Spirit-Matter, and that they exist on all five levels of our world. Scientists will call it "spiritualized Matter," while metaphysicians will call it "materialised Spirit." It doesn't matter which term you use as long as you remember that both are always present in every manifestation and that what you see is not just the play of matter but also the play of Spirit through Matter. Then, when you read an old book and come across the phrase "mind is material," you won't be confused. You'll know that the author is just speaking on the

Samkhyan line, which talks about Matter everywhere but always implies that the Spirit is watching and that this presence makes Matter's work possible. You won't get the opposite view of materialists, which says "mind is the product of matter," mixed up with the Indian philosophy that says "mind is material." They are two very different ideas. The Samkhyan may use materialistic language, but he always believes in the energising power of Spirit. A materialist, on the other hand, sees Spirit as something that comes from Matter. There is a big gap between them, even though they may speak the same language most of the time.

Mind

"Yoga is the stopping of the mind's functions," says Patanjali. It is necessary to turn off the mind's processes. To fully understand what this means, let us look more closely at what the Indian philosopher means by the word "mind."

There are three main things that make up the mind in a broad sense: the ability to think, the wish or will to act, and the ability to perceive. Yoga doesn't deal with all three of these right away; it only deals with the third, which is thought, or the Samkhyan subject. As we've seen, though, you can't fully separate cognition from the others because consciousness is a whole. Even though we're only interested in the part of consciousness that we call cognition, we can't get it by itself. So, the Indian psychologist who is studying this trait, cognition, divides it into three parts, or four parts as the Vedanta says (I agree with the Vedantin that this is wrong). A word that literally means "internal organ" is used to describe the mind in any Vedantic book that talks about it. This word, antah-karana, is always used where "mind" is used in English. However, it is only used to talk about thought, not action or desire. It's said to be fourfold, with Manas, Buddhi, Ahamkara, and Chitta making it up. But this fourfold split is very strange. What is Chitta? We know what Manas, Buddhi, and Ahamkara are. Outside of Manas, Buddhi, and Ahamkara, what is Chitta? Choose whoever you want, writing down his answer will show you that it is very general. Let's look at it ourselves and see if the Theosophical idea of a triplet summed up in a fourth, which isn't really a fourth but the sum of the three, sheds any light on it. There are three sides to a triangle, and they are called Manas, Buddhi, and Ahamkara. Not a fourth, but the sum of the first three: Manas, Buddhi, and Ahamkara. This is an old idea of a trio that is one. H. P. Blavatsky always adds this total as a fourth to her triplets because she still uses the old ways. This fourth one, which combines the first three but is not different from them, brings them together even though they seem to be different. Now let's use that with Antahkarana.

Take notice. That part of the Self is most present in cognition, but it can't live by itself; the whole Self is present in all acts of cognition. The same thing goes for the other two. It is impossible for one to live without the others. Where there is cognition, the other two are also there, but they are less important than cognition. There is intention and action. If we imagine the purest form of knowledge, which is itself, then we have Buddhi, which is pure reason and the core of knowledge. In the universe, Vishnu stands for this, as the universe's sustaining wisdom. Now let us think of cognition as looking outwards and reflecting itself in activity, which is its brother quality. This mix of cognition and activity is called Manas, the active mind. In people, Manas is activity, and in the world, Brahma is activity reflecting cognition. When thought shows up in will in the same way, it's called Ahamkara, which means "I am I" in human language and is represented by Mahadeva in the world. So far, we've found three divisions that make up the internal organ or Antahkarana: Manas, Buddhi, and Ahamkara. We haven't been able to find a fourth. Okay, so what is Chitta? Is the sum of the three, or the sum of the three things put together. Because of the old way of keeping track of these things, Antahkarana is split into four parts.

Intellectual Being

Now we need to talk about the mental body, which is basically the same thing as the mind. In practical yoga, the first thing a man needs to do is remove himself from his mental body by pulling away from it and into the sheath above it. And now remember what I said before: in Yoga, the Self is always the consciousness + the vehicle that the consciousness can't separate itself from. For practical reasons, the only thing above the body you can't leave is the Self. Your first step should be to separate yourself from your mental body. In these situations, Manas must be linked to the Self, and the spiritual trio (Atma, Buddha, and Manas) must be seen as different from the mental body. That's the first thing to do. You need to be able to pick up and put down your mind like you would a tool before you can think about how the Self can get rid of its bags even more. Because of this, the mind body is where we begin. Hold your thoughts in. Put it down. Keep it up. What is the normal state of the mind body now? When you look down at that person from above, you can see that the colours are always changing. You find that they start from inside and outside the group at times. There have been times when a vibration from outside has changed awareness and the colours in the mental body have changed to match. It is thought that when awareness changes, it makes the matter that consciousness is working in vibrate. The mental body is made up of hues and colours that are always changing. It is never still and changes colour very quickly all over.

All of these things can be stopped by yoga, along with energy and changes. If you stop the change in consciousness, the mental body stops vibrating. If you check the mental body's vibration, you check the change in consciousness. If a Master's mind is completely under control, no outside stimulation can cause any answer or vibration. There is no change in colour in that mind unless it comes from within. The coloured mind of a Master is like moonlight on the ocean that is moving. There are all sorts of colours inside that white, moon-like brightness, but nothing in the outside world can make even the tiniest change in colour cover its steady shine. If there is a change in awareness inside, it will send a wave of soft colours through the mental body, which only reacts with colour to changes that come from inside and never from outside. The mind that he has is never Himself; it's just a tool that He can use or leave behind whenever He wants. He only uses the outside sheath when He needs to talk to the lower world.

Inhibition means that all changes of colour in the mental body stop. This helps you understand what it means. In yoga, the mind's processes are turned off. First, you need to work on your mind. You need to learn how to stop all of those movements and make your mental body colourless, still, and quiet, only responding to the commands you give it. How will you know when your mind is truly under control and not a part of you anymore? This will become clear to you when you learn that you can stop the flow of thought and keep your mind completely still with your will. One sheath after another has to be overcome, and you know you've done it when it stops affecting you. It can't change you, but you can change it. When there is nothing outside of you that can bother you or move your mind, when your mind only reacts to things outside of you on its own, then you can say, "This is not my Self." Since it is now part of the outside world, it is no longer the same as the Self.

In the same way, this leads to the capture of the causal body. It is time to move on to the Buddhaic body after you have fully controlled the causing body. You move on to conquering the Atmic body once you have mastered the Buddhic body.

Mindfulness and Individual Being

Being in a situation where functions keep going away shouldn't surprise you when the poor student asks, "What becomes of the mind itself?" What's left if you turn off all the functions?" When things get hard in the Indian way of teaching, someone steps up and asks a question. And the question that makes things harder is always asked in the comments. This is what Patanjali said: "Then the observer stays in his own form." The answer from Theosophy is "The Monad remains." It's the end of the journey of people. That is the highest point that people can reach: to stop all the reflections in the fivefold universe that the Monad has used to show his powers, and then for the Monad to know himself, better for having gone through the experiences that his shown parts have had. But for the Samkhyan, the problem is very big, because when there is only one viewer left, the spectator almost disappears when the show is over. He had no job other than to watch the mind games. What's left when the mind games are over? He is no longer able to watch because there is nothing to see. "He stays in his own form" is the only answer. He can no longer manifest because he has crossed over into the other side of duality. The Spirit then sinks back into delay and can no longer manifest. This is where your view of the world differs very much from the Theosophical view. In the Theosophical view, when all of these functions are turned off, the Monad rules over matter and is ready for a new cycle of activity, no longer a slave but a master.

It is clear from all the comparisons that the Self does not lose ground in Self-realization as it pulls away from each sheath. Instead, he gets it. Self-realization gets clearer with each withdrawal. As the Self peels back one layer of matter after another, he or she realises that each body is not themselves. This process of withdrawal makes the Self's sense of reality stronger, not weaker. It is important to remember this because when Westerners read about Eastern ideas, they often confuse the state of liberation, also known as Nirvana, with nothingness or unconsciousness. This is a huge mistake that can affect how they think about all Yogic processes. Imagine a man who links himself with his body so much that he can't separate himself from it, not even in his thoughts. This is the state of an early, undeveloped man. Now, compare that to the strength, vigour, and clarity of your own mental consciousness.

The early man's awareness was limited to his body, with only brief glimpses of dream consciousness. It had a very small range. He doesn't know how big your mind is or how vague your thoughts are. Are the early man's thoughts more or less clear than yours, though? You will definitely say that it is less vivid. You have mostly gone beyond his conscious abilities. Your awareness is astral instead of physical, which has made it more vivid. While the Self is pulling away from each sheath, he sees himself more and more, not less and less. As each sheath is thrown away, self-realization gets stronger. At some point, the centre will know itself at every point of the circumference. As the circle gets less dense, the centre will become stronger. Once that is done, the centre stays the same but the circumference goes away. The centre is still there. You are more vividly aware than early man, and your awareness is more alive than that of an undeveloped man. The same is true for us as we move up the life stairs and discard one layer after another. Being more aware of our presence, our knowledge, and our self-determined power makes us more aware. More and more of the Self's qualities become clear as each veil falls away. For the same reason, our awareness should be stronger, clearer, and better when we touch the Monad. Your forces and emotions get stronger as you learn to live.

Also, keep in mind that all power is held over sheaths, which are parts of the Not-Self. You don't have control over your Self; you have control over your Not-Self. The Self can't be controlled; He is the Inner Ruler who will never die. He is in charge, not being ruled. You will understand that the Upanishad is true when each sheath gives way to your Self and each body becomes a tool for your Self. At that point, you will be the Self, the Inner Ruler, and the eternal.

Chapter 3
Yoga from a Scientific Viewpoint

I'd like to start by talking about the two most important types of yoga: one that deals with the Self and the other with the Not-Self. Before I start, I want to tell you that we are only talking about the science of Yoga and not about other ways to become one with God. I want you to pay attention to the scientific method, which is based on an old Indian idea. Of course, I should tell you that Bhakti and Karma are also great ways to live your life. This is just one of them. As with everything in nature, the yoga we are learning is mainly about the Marga of Jnanam, or knowledge. And within that Marga, or path of knowledge, we find three subdivisions.

Yoga Disciplines

I just talked about what I called the "two great methods" in yoga. One of them leads to knowledge through Buddhi, or pure reason, and the other leads to knowledge through Manas, or the concrete mind. You may remember that when I talked about the different parts of Antah-karana yesterday, I said that each one was a reflection of a different quality. For example, in the cognitional part of the Self, there is Buddhi, which is cognition reflected in cognition; Ahamkara, which is cognition reflected in will; and Manas, which is cognition reflected in activity. Keeping these three sub-groups in mind, it will be easy to see that these two types of yoga naturally fit into two of them. What about the third? What about the will? Ahamkara is the spirit of will in thought. That does have some good points, but it's not really a "method." The will breaks its way up by being completely determined, keeping its eyes on the end goal and not caring whether it uses buddha or manes to get there. Metaphysics is used to understand the Not-Self and science is used to understand the Self, but both are understood and then thrown away depending on what is needed at the time. People whose will is strong often don't know how they get what they want; it just comes to them; they wanted it, and nature gave it to them. In Yoga, this can be seen in the man of Ahamkara, which is a type of will in thought. As Ahamkara and Manas are subordinate in the man of Ahamkara, Ahamkara and Manas are also subordinate in the man of Buddhi. Ahamkara and Buddhi are present in the man of Manas, but they play a supporting role. Ahamkara has to back up both the metaphysician and the science. Self-determination, or putting yourself on purpose to reach a goal, is an important part of all types of yoga. If a Yogi wants to follow the path of Buddhi, which is all about thinking, or the path of Manas, which is more about doing things, he needs to have self-determining will to help him get through his hard work. You may remember that the Upanishad says a weak person can't reach the Self. People want strength. People want to know what to do. We want you to keep going. And just like any great yogi, you must have that intense determination that makes you unique.

So, what are these two great ways? One of them could be called "seeking the Self by the Self," and the other could be called "seeking the Self by the Not-Self." If you think about them that way, I think the idea will help you. People who seek the Self by the Self do so through the power of buddhi. They always look inside and stay away from the outside world. People who look for the Self through the Not-Self do so through the active working Manas. They are turned outward, and studying the Not-Self helps them discover the Self. One is the path of the philosopher, and the other is the path of the science.

Inward Journey of the Self

We should use the right tools to look at this a little more closely. It was already said that the way of the metaphysician is where the faculty of Buddhi is most often used. It's the way of the philosopher. He looks inside himself, always trying to find the Self by exploring the deepest parts of himself. He tries to take off one layer of clothing and one package at a time because he knows that the Self is inside him. As he rejects them, he reaches the glory of the unveiled Self. In order to do this, he needs to stop thinking in specific terms and start living in more general terms.

So, his way must be hard, long-lasting, and patient meditation. In order to reach his goal, he must think very hard and quickly. This will help him move from the concrete to the abstract parts of his mind, and then from the abstract parts of his mind to the part where he can sense unity. He must keep thinking very hard and quickly until Buddhi opens up into Atma and the Self can be seen in all his glory, with only a thin layer of atmic matter remaining as an envelope. That tough and difficult road is where you must go to find the Self by way of the Self.

This kind of man must not care about the Not-Self at all. He needs to shut out the rest of the world. He can't be touched by anyone or anything anymore. He has to close his senses to all the vibrations that come from outside, and he has to ignore all the different things that make up the universe of the Not-Self. He will feel better if he is alone until he is strong enough to close himself off from outside influences. There is a good place for this road in the Roman Catholic Church's contemplative orders. The outside world was pushed as far away as possible. It's a trap, a temptation, and a mess. The Yogi must always turn away from the world and focus on the Self. So, for people who walk this path, the so-called Siddhis are direct problems, not solutions. But the statement that the Siddhis are bad is much broader than some current Theosophists think. People who say that you should avoid the Siddhis forget that the Indian who says that also doesn't use their physical senses. He shuts his eyes and ears because they get in the way. But some Theosophists say that you shouldn't use your mental or spirit senses at all. They don't mind if you use your physical senses, though, and they don't think that they are obstacles. What's the harm? If the senses are problems in their tinier forms, they are also problems in their bigger forms. For a person who wants to find the Self by the Self, every sense is an impediment. It makes no sense to give up only the more subtle senses while forgetting about the physical senses' desires, which are just as much an impediment as the others. A person trying to understand the world around them doesn't have to worry about such a divide. Everything that isn't Self is a hurdle in the search for the Self by the Self. Everything that connects you to the outside world—your eyes, ears, and other senses—is an obstacle. The more subtle forms of these senses that connect you to the astral and mental worlds of matter are also an obstacle. This extreme fear of the Siddhis is just a reaction, not based on understanding but on a lack of understanding. And people who say bad things about the Siddhis should follow the lead of a Hindu Yogi or a Roman Catholic recluse, who say all the senses and their objects are bad and in the way. As the physical senses and other brain functions become more acute, many Theosophists in the West and here believe that much is gained. However, as soon as the senses become astral or the brain functions start to work in astral matter, they see these things as bad and condemn them. That doesn't make sense. It doesn't make sense. Any senses, whether you call them Siddhis or not, get in the way of your search for the Self by making you turn away from the Not-Self.

The person who wants to find the Self by finding the Self must have "faith" in the sense that I previously described it: a deep, strong belief that the Self within you is real and that nothing can change that. That's the only thing that could be called holy in the name of faith. It really goes against reason, because the Self can't be known to be real through reason. Really, it's not based on argument, because you can't find your Self through reason. It's the Self inside you testifying to his own supreme truth, and you need to have that unwavering belief, or shraddha, to walk this path. It's important because without it, the difficulties of seeking the Self would break people's minds, their courage, and their determination. But the strong belief that the Self is the only thing that can comfort the pilgrim in the darkness that falls on him and the void that he must cross before the life of the lower is lost and the life of the higher comes to life. For a Yogi on this path, this strong faith is like knowledge and experience for a Yogi on the other path.

Inner Awakening via External Experience

From him, turn to the person who wants to find the Self through the Not-Self. There is a way for a scientist to use the concrete, active Manas to understand the world scientifically. He has to find the real among the unreal, the eternal among the changing, and the Self among the many forms. What should he do? By hard and thorough study of all the different shapes and sizes that the Self has hidden himself. So he has to study the Not-Self around him and in himself, figure out his own nature, analyse to understand, study nature in others and in himself, get to know himself and others better, and keep going until he reaches the top. He has to do this slowly, step by step, plane by plane, turning down each form of matter because it's not the Self he's looking for. He uses his most powerful senses to understand and then reject as he learns to master the physical plane. "This is not my Self," he says. It's clear that this shifting view, these obscurities, and these constant changes are the opposite of the Self's stability, clarity, and infinity. "These can't be my Self." Because of this, he always turns them down. He goes to the astral plane and uses the better astral senses to study the astral world. But the astral world is also changing, and it doesn't show how the Self is not changing. Following the path of forms, he goes from the astral world to the mental plane and studies the Manasic world's ever-changing forms, only to reject them again: "These are not the Self." He then goes even higher, always following the path of forms, to the Buddhic plane, where the Self starts to show his beauty and brightness in manifested union. In this way, learning diversity leads him to the idea of unity, which leads him to the understanding of the One. For him, understanding the Self comes from studying the Not-Self and separating it from the Self. This means that he does what the other person does with faith and pure thought. In order to find the Self through the Not-Self, you need what are called Siddhis. You can't study the mental or astral worlds without the mental or astral senses, just like you can't study the real world without the physical senses. So, pick your goals calmly and then think about how to get there. Then you won't have any trouble deciding what method to use or which road to take.

So we can see that there are two ways to do things. You should keep these two ways separate in your mind. You can get to the Self by following the philosophical line of pure thought. In the same way, you can reach the Self along the line of science experimentation and observation—the physical line in the broadest sense of the word. Each is a way to do Yoga. Reading the Yoga Sutras of Patanjali will tell you how to do both of these things. There will be no more contradictions between those ways if you separate them in your mind. In the later parts of his Sutras, Patanjali gives some hints about how the Siddhis can be grown. This is one way to get to the Supreme.

Yoga and Morality

The next thing I want you to think about is that yoga is a branch of psychology. I also want to make it clear that it is not a science of ethics, even though ethics is what it is based on. Ethics and psychology are not the same thing. The study of the mind led to the development of the field of psychology. As a result of studying how people should behave so that they can get along with each other, the field of ethics was created. It is not an investigation into the nature of mind or the ways that mind powers can be grown and evolved. Ethics is the study of life. At this point, I'm taking a break because many people are confused about this. Such a mess shouldn't happen if you know what Yoga is all about. People get the wrong idea when they think that they have to find what are called "precepts of morality" or "ethics" in Yoga. The first two angas of Yoga by Patanjali talk about the universal rules of morality and right behaviour. These rules are called yama and niyama. However, they are not the main topic; they are just the basis of it. It goes without saying that you can't do yoga if you don't have the moral qualities put up in yama and niyama. That being said, you shouldn't expect to find moral rules in a science psychology book like Yoga. If someone studies the science of electricity and doesn't find any moral rules in it, that doesn't surprise them. So why should someone studying Yoga, which is the study of psychology, think that they will find moral rules in it? I'm not saying that the Yogi doesn't care about morals. Not at all, it is very important. It is a must for everyone in the beginning stages of yoga. If a Yogi has learned these, though, he doesn't have to do them if he wants to go left. Remember that there is a Yoga of the left-hand path and a Yoga of the right-hand path. Asceticism is always present in the early stages and sometimes in the later ones, but there is no real morals. Yoga comes next. Most of the time, the black magician has the same strict morals as any Brother of the White Lodge.The words "while" and "black" in this sentence have nothing to do with race or colour. People who follow the black magician are more likely to be religious than those who follow the white magician. He is not trying to clean up life for the sake of humanity. Instead, he wants to clean up the car so that he can get power more easily. The white magician and the black magician are different in what they want to do. A white magician who follows the right path might not want to eat meat because the way they get it goes against the law of kindness. People who follow the left way may also not eat meat, but for a different reason: his vehicle would not work as well if it were full of the rajasic parts of meat. The reason is what makes them different. The motion on the outside is the same. If you only look at what they do, you could say that both guys are moral. The goal shows the way, but the acts are often the same on the outside.

For some, not eating meat is moral because it reduces the pain of others. However, from a yogic point of view, not eating meat is not a moral act but only a way to reach a goal. Some of the most important yogis in Hindu writing were and still are men who you would correctly call black magicians. They are still yogis, though. Ravana, the anti-Christ and the Avatara of evil, was one of the best yogis ever. He gathered all the bad things in the world into himself to fight the Avatara of good. He was a great and wonderful yogi, and he got his strength from yoga. Ravana was a typical yogi on the left path. He was a great destroyer, and he did yoga to get the power to destroy so that he could take the Planetary Logos's blessing that no one could kill him. "What a strange thing that a man can force God to give him such power," you might say. God speaks through the laws of nature, and if a person follows a law of nature, he will get what that law guarantees. It doesn't matter if he is good or bad to other people; this is a separate issue. It doesn't matter what other law is followed or not followed. There is no doubt that the scientific man can be moral or immoral, as long as his sin doesn't affect his ears, eyes, or brain. The same goes for Yoga. Even though morality is very important, it doesn't have anything to do with these things. If you think it does, you'll always be changing your moral position, either making it less important or making it seem silly. Theosophists should try to understand. Once you understand, you won't make the same mistakes or be as confused as other people do when they think that laws from one part of the world will cause things to happen in another. That's clear to the scientific man. He is aware that making a science discovery has nothing to do with how good he is, so he wouldn't think about doing something nice to find a new element. No matter how bad his personal life is, he will never fail at a well-planned project. The things are in different places, and he doesn't mix up the rules of those places.

Ishvara is completely fair, so a person who follows a law will reap the benefits of that law, even if their deeds in other areas are not good for people. You will get rice if you plant rice and weeds if you plant weeds. The harvest is based on what was sown. For this is a world of rules. The law helps us win and take over. So where does morals fit in? When you deal with a right-hand path magician, also known as a servant of the White Lodge, morals is the most important thing. Because he is learning to be a servant of humanity, he must follow the highest morals, not just the morality of the world. This is because the white magician's job is to help people get along with each other. The white artist needs to wait. The evil witch doctor might be mean. The white magician must care about people, because caring about others makes him a better person, and he's trying to include everyone in his awareness. But not for the bad guy. He has the freedom to ignore kindness.

It is possible for a white wizard to want power. His goal when he wants power is to serve people and make himself more useful to them, making him a better worker in the service of the world. But not for the dark side brother. He wants power for himself so that he can use it against everyone else. He might be mean and rude. He wants to be alone, and being mean and rude tends to make that happen. He wants power, and it's possible for him to briefly go against the Divine Will in evolution in order to get that power.

Nirvana is the end of the one, where there is no more divide. Avichi, the utmost solitude, is the end of the other. It is the kaivalya of the black wizard. Both of them are yogis and follow the science of yoga. They both get the result of the law they followed: one gets the kaivalya of Nirvana and the other gets the kaivalya of Avichi.

Structure of Mental States

This is where the "states of the mind" come in. Patanjali used the word Vritti to talk about the different states of mind. This beautifully put together language, Sanskrit, tells you what a word means right there. Vrittis means the mind's "being" or the different ways it can exist. It can also mean the mind's modes of existence or the ways it exists. That's what this word really means. "Going around" or "moving in a circle" is a secondary meaning. In yoga, you have to stop every way of being that your mind shows itself. You are told that these mental states are made up of five different parts in order to help you learn how to stop them. This is because you can't stop them until you understand them. They have five dots. The standard translation of the Sutra is that it says "the Vrittis are fivefold (panchatayyah)," but pentad is a better way to read the word pancha-tayyah in the original. Chemists talk about a monad, triad, or heptad when they are working with elements. The word "pentad" makes you think of those terms right away. Different things that the scientist works with are connected to the unit-element in different ways. It has elements that are related to it in one way only. These are called monads. Elements that are related in two ways are called duads, and so on.

Can this also be used for states of mind? It is said in a shloka of the Bhagavad-Gita that when the Jiva goes out into the world, he brings with him the mind as the sixth sense. That might help explain things a bit. You know things in five different ways, or jnanendriyas, which are your five senses. You can only know the outside world through these five senses. According to Western psychology, there is nothing in thought that is not present in experience. That isn't always true; it's not always true of the real mind or the abstract mind. But there is a lot of truth to it. There are six ideas in all. It's made up of five parts. The idea is made up of five different parts, each of which comes from a different sense. In the end, each thought will have seven parts, or heptads. There are five things about each present that make up the idea. The mind brings everything together into a single thought and joins the five senses. As you think about an orange, you will notice that it has colour, which you get from your eyes, a scent, which you get from your nose, a taste, which you get from your tongue, and a roughness or smoothness, which you get from your touch. If your hearing were sharper, you would hear musical notes made by the vibrations of the molecules. If you could hear nothing at all. Anywhere there is energy, there is sound. So you would also hear the orange. The mind has put all of this together into one thought, which is an orange. That's what the "association of ideas" is all about. A scent not only makes you think of the place and time when it was smelled, but also because all five senses are involved in making an effect, so when one is stimulated, the others are brought back to mind. The mind works like a lens. Put a prism in the way of a white light ray, and it will split into its seven parts. This will make seven colours appear. Place another prism in front of these seven rays. As they go through the prism, the order of the steps changes, and the seven appear as a single white light. The second lens is the mind. The five sense impressions are brought in and put together into a single principal. As things stand, there are only five senses left, so this brings the five feelings together into one thought. The white ray is to the seven-colored light what an idea or thought is to the five-senses. "Vrittayah panchatayych," which means "the vrittis, or modes of the mind, are pentads," means exactly this. The next lessons will be easier to understand if you look at it that way.

As I already said, that statement is not entirely true. It says that there is nothing in thought that is not in sensation. If you have the sixth sense, manas, it adds its own pure natural nature to the feelings. What species do you think was added in this way? When the mind adds something, it really just sets up a relationship. All thinking is the "establishment of relations," and the more you think about that phrase, the more you'll see that it refers to all the different things that the mind does. The mind's first action is to become aware of the world around it. We become aware of something outside of ourselves, even if it's only slightly at first. This is usually called perception. When I talk about brain processes, I use the more general term "establishing a relation," while perception only refers to one thing. To use a common metaphor, a baby feels pain when a pin is stuck in its skin, but it doesn't know what the pin is or where it is at first. It can't figure out what part of the body the pin is in. Perception means connecting a feeling with the thing that makes the feeling happen. So, there is no perception. For scientific purposes, you only "perceive" something when you connect yourself to it. That is the very first of these brain processes. It comes right after how we feel. From an Eastern point of view, sensation is also a mental function, since the senses are part of the reasoning faculty. However, in Western psychology, they are mistakenly grouped with feelings. Now that you've created that link between yourself and things outside, what does the mind do next? That is, reasoning is the process of setting up relationships between different things, just like sight is the process of setting up your relationship with a single thing. Once you have seen a lot of things, you start to use logic to figure out how they are related. Reasoning is the creation of a new relationship, which comes from comparing different things that you have already perceived in relation to yourself. This creates an idea. Simply putting this word together, "establishment of relations," describes everything. Setting up relationships is an important part of thinking, which makes sense since the Supreme Thinker created matter by setting up a relationship. By creating that first connection between Himself and the Not-Self, He makes the universe possible. In the same way, we mirror His powers in ourselves by thinking in the same way, making connections, and doing all intellectual processes in this way.

Bliss and Agony

Let's go back to something else this great yoga teacher said: "There are two kinds of pentads: painful and non-painful." Not saying "painful and pleasant" makes no sense. He saw things clearly and logically, and he uses the logical split that includes all of discourse, such as A and Not-A, painful and not-painful. Many scientists disagree about a third type: "indifferent." Some scientists say that there are three types of feelings: painful, pleasant, and indifferent. Pain and joy aren't the only types of feelings. There's also indifference, which is neither painful nor pleasant. A different school of psychology says that indifference is just pain or happiness that isn't clear enough to be called one or the other. Now, psychologists might not be in this mess and debate if the main division of feelings was a logical division. Only "A" and "Not-A" make sense as a split. In every way, Patanjali makes sense and is right. He separates all vrittis, or ways of thinking, into painful and nonpainful ones so that he doesn't fall into the same trap as modern psychologists.

But there is a psychological reason to say "pleasure and pain," even though it doesn't make sense. The reason for this grouping is that the words "pleasure" and "pain" describe two basic states of difference, not in the self but in the things that the self lives in. The Self is naturally limitless, so any limits that try to put him in a box are always pushing against him. We feel "pain" when these limits push back against the steady pressure of the Self, and "pleasure" when they give in a little. Actually, these states aren't so much of the Self as they are of the vehicles and of certain changes in awareness. Pain and pleasure are part of the Self as a whole, not of any one part of the Self. Once it is clear that pleasure and pain are only part of the desire nature, the objection is raised: "Well, but there is intense pleasure in using the cognitive faculty." Feeling a deep sense of joy when using the creative part of your mind is a completely different thing from wanting something. The correct answer is "Pleasure is part of the Self as a whole." Being "pleasured" happens when the cars give way to the Self and let it "expand," which is what it always does. People are right when they say, "Pleasure is a sense of moreness." You'll find that the word "moreness" fits every time you feel good. The pleasure of eating will be covered, since it is the lowest form of joy. As you take food from the Not-Self and use it for yourself, you become more. It is true of the greatest state of happiness, which is union with the Supreme. As you grow to His infinite size, you become more. When a word can be used for both the smallest and largest things, you can be pretty sure it covers everything. This means that "pleasure is moreness" is a true statement. Pain is also "lessness."

If you know these things, your life theory will make more sense, and you'll be better able to help people who are going bad. Do something to help you. One of the best things about drinking is that it makes life seem more sharp and lively in the beginning. That point is crossed by the man who gets drunk, and then the draw stops. The first steps are what make it so appealing, and a lot of people who would never get drunk have been there. Viewers who drink wine become more chatty and active. This is what makes it interesting and dangerous.

Most coarse kinds of excess are appealing because they make you feel more alive, and you can't save a man from his excess unless you know why he does it. When you know what makes the first step, which is more life, appealing, you can find the point of temptation and use that in your case with him. This kind of mental study is not only interesting, but it can also help anyone who wants to help people. Understanding makes it easier for you to help others.

That brings up the next question: "Why doesn't he divide all feelings into pleasurable and not-pleasurable instead of "painful and not-painful"?" "Oh, the Hindu is naturally so pessimistic that he naturally ignores pleasure and talks about painful and not-painful," is a response that most Westerners will know. All of space and time is painful. Although that's not the right answer. Firstly, a Hindu is not negative. He certainly has the most positive outlook. Every single school of philosophy that he knows of puts the goal of philosophy at the top of its list of things to do. However, he is very logical. He knows we don't have to look for happiness. As such, it is already ours because it is who we are. The Upanishads say, "The Self is bliss." You are always and forever happy. It is the way you normally are. Don't go looking for it. You will always be happy if you get rid of the things that are holding you back, which are called pain. Pain is more important than happiness, and those painful things need to be gotten rid of. As soon as they stop, you must be glad. So Patanjali says, "The vrittis are both painful and not painful." Pain is a waste product. That thing will not last. The Self, which is bliss, is the life of the whole world, so pain has no place in it. The Hindu view is the most positive in the world.

Allow us to ponder for a moment: "If the Self is bliss, then why is there any pain?" The reason for this is that the Self is happiness. If only streams of happiness came into the Self, he would not be able to turn outward and become real. He wouldn't have been aware of the streams. You couldn't add anything to the endless happiness. If there were no obstacles in the way of a stream of water, adding more water would not delay the flow; the stream would continue as it was. However, if you put something in the way, the stream will fight and fume against the thing that is in the way and do everything it can to sweep it away. What goes against it, what stops the smooth flow of its current, is the only thing that will make it work. That is the first thing pain does. The Self can only be awakened by this. The only thing that can get his attention is that. When the peaceful, happy, sleeping, inverted Self feels the pain surge against him, he wakes up and asks, "What is this? It goes against my nature and I find it disgusting." It awakens him to the idea that there is a universe, or outer world, around him. According to psychology and yoga, pain is the most important thing for realising oneself because it pushes oneself to do things that aren't related to oneself. So, when our commentator talks about pain, he says that all painful experiences are built by the causal body, which is where all the seeds of karma are stored. This leads us to the big idea: the first job of pain in the universe is to make the Self active by making him aware of the outside world.

The next thing pain does is organise the cars. Pain makes a person work hard, and as he does that, the parts of his cars slowly start to fit together better. To shape and grow your muscles, you have to work at it and work them out. This brings more life into them and makes them strong. The Self needs pain to push his vehicles to work hard in ways that improve and order them. So pain not only makes us aware, it also sets up the cars.

It also does something else. The pain cleans. Things that hurt us are things we try to get rid of. It goes against who we are, and we try to get rid of it. Pain shakes out of the vehicles everything that isn't in line with the Self's joyful nature. Over time, the vehicles become clean through suffering and are then ready to handle the Self.

There is a fourth use for it. Pain can teach. A lot of the best lessons in life are learned through pain, not happiness. As I get older, I think about the long life I've lived, which has been full of storms, stress, problems, and hard work. This makes me think of the great lessons that pain can teach us. If I could erase all the joy and happiness from my life story without feeling bad about it, I would not let go of a single pain, because pain is what makes us wise.

There is a fifth use for it. Feeling pain makes you strong. After writing about the fights and overthrows in his great poem "Time and Satan," Edward Carpenter said, "Every pain that I suffered in one body became a power that I wielded in the next." Changed pain is power.

Since wise people know these things, they don't run away from pain because they know it leads to purity, knowledge, and power.

It is possible for a person to be in so much pain that it numbs them to the world and makes them useless for this life. This is especially true when the pain was too much as a child. But even then, he will get his good harvest in the end. Because of his past, he may have to go through pain now, but he can still turn it into a golden chance by understanding and using its power.

You might ask, "Then what's the point of pleasure if pain is so wonderful?" From happiness comes light. Pleasure makes the Self appear. In joy, all of the Self's vehicles are in sync with each other; they all vibrate at the same time. The vibrations are rhythmic, not jumbled like they are in pain, and they allow the Self to grow, which leads to illumination, or knowing the Self. That is true, so you will see that happiness is a very important part of nature because it is part of the Self and belongs to him. When it aligns the cars of the Self from the outside, it makes it easier for the Self to show up through our lower selves. Because of this, happiness is a state of light. This is why the delight of the mystic is so valuable: it is a deep joy. He is filled with a huge wave of happiness that comes from love triumphing. This huge wave of happiness harmonises all of his bodies, both subtle and gross, and makes the glory of the Self visible. He also sees the face of his God. Then there is the beautiful light, which temporarily blocks out all the lower worlds. Because the Self considers himself holy for a moment, he can see the divine aspect of himself. So you shouldn't be afraid of happiness any more than you are of pain, as some foolish people do because of their wrong religious beliefs. It's a common mistake in religious people to think that happiness is something to be feared, as if God didn't want His children to be happy. This is one of the nightmares that come from not knowing enough and being scared. Phenomenon of life is happiness. When God is joy, He can't hold a grudge against His children. Every bit of joy in the world is a reflection of the Divine Life and the Self in the middle of matter. So, both happiness and pain serve a purpose, and the wise person welcomes that because they know it and can use it. Along this line, it's easy to see how both pleasure and pain become acceptable. The wise man doesn't identify with either, so he just takes either as it comes, knowing what it's for. It's easier to deal with both happiness and sadness when we know where they come from. We exploit pain when it appears. Feeling happy is something we take and use. So we can go through life accepting both happiness and sadness, being happy with whatever comes our way and not wanting what isn't there right now. In this way, we can reach a higher level of indifference than the stoic, to the true vairagya. Both joy and pain are transcended, and the Self, who is bliss, stays.

Chapter 4
The Practice of Yoga

When I talked about the third part of the topic, I brought up the states of mind and told you that the word vritti in Samskrit means "ways in which the mind exists." In other words, these states of mind are modes of mind, or ways in which the mind exists. These are the states that need to be stopped, gotten rid of, or brought down to complete silence. Creating a state that lets the higher mind pour itself into the lower mind is what this block is for. Or, to put it another way, the calm, steady lower mind reflects the higher mind like a still lake reflects the stars. You will remember the phrase from the Upanishad that says, "In the peace of the mind and the calm of the senses, a man may see the majesty of the Self." This phrase is less technical and scientific and more beautiful. What we need to think about now is how to bring about this peace.

Suppression of Emotional States

It is possible to stop these modes, or ways of being, of the mind in just two ways. Sri Krishna gave them to Arjuna in the Bhagavad-Gita when he said that the mind was as strong, quick, hard to control, and bend as the wind. Without a doubt, O strong-armed, the mind is restless and hard to control. But it can be controlled by steady practice (abhyasa) and by not caring about anything (vai-ragya).

These are the only two ways to calm this mind down after it has been racing and storming. Vai-ragya and abhyasa are the only two ways to get there, but they always work when performed regularly.

Let's think about what these two well-known words mean. Vai-ragya, which means "dispassion," means getting rid of all passion and attraction for the things that we feel. It also means breaking the bonds of desire that hold us to the things around us. Raga means "passion, addiction," or what holds a man to things. By grammar rules, the word "vi" changes to "vai," which means "without" or "opposite to." So vai-ragya means "non-passion, absence of passion," and it has nothing to do with any of these outside things. Remembering that thought is the process of making connections, we can see that getting rid of connections will make the mind still, which is what Yoga is all about. Every raga has to be thrown out. Let's get away from it. We need to reach the opposite state, where all passions are stilled, where there is no longer any draw to the things we want, and where all the bonds that hold a person to the things around him are broken. "A person is immortal when the bonds of the heart are broken."

How is it that this lack of emotion will be achieved? There is just one right way to do it. By slowly pulling ourselves away from things in the outside world through the stronger pull of the Self. The Self is always drawn to itself. That attraction is all that can keep these vehicles away from the attractive and repulsive objects around them. When the separated Self is freed from all raga and no longer has to create relationships with objects, he is set free and free, and union with the one Self becomes his only desire. But this great quality of objectivity can't become the trait of a man who is set on Yoga right away, by one supreme effort, by one attempt. He has to practise being impartial all the time. That's what the word means when it's joined with dispassion, abhyasa, or practice. The practice has to go on all the time and not stop. "Practice" doesn't just mean meditation, even though that's how the word is usually used. It also means doing something without emotion while being surrounded by things that make you feel good.

When you want to become dispassionate, you have to use it in your daily life. I already said that a lot of people limit abhyasa to meditation. That's why not many people get to Yoga. Another mistake is to wait for a big chance to come up. People get ready to make a huge sacrifice and forget about the little things that happen every day. The mind is connected to things through a million tiny threads. These small things don't get our attention because they're not important, and while people wait for the big thing that doesn't come, they forget to be objective about the little things that are happening around them every day. When we stop wanting things all the time, we stop caring about the things around us. Then, when the big chance comes up, we take it without even realising it. Anyone who wants to learn Yoga has to practise every day, all day long, because that's the only way to get better. And most people who want to learn Yoga give up because it's so hard to keep doing it.

I need to warn you about a threat. There is a rough way to quickly make people not care about anything. Some people tell you, "Kill all love and affection; harden your hearts; become cold to everyone around you; leave your wife, kids, parents, and fly to the desert or the jungle; build a wall between yourself and everything you want; then you will be dispassionate." It is true that is a pretty easy way to become dispassionate. But that kills more than it wants. You built a wall around the Self, which is love, that he can't get through. You make it hard to move by putting up a thick shell around yourself that you can't break through. It's because you harden yourself when you should be softened and separate yourself when you should be embracing others. You kill love along with desire, forgetting that love clings to the Self and seeks the Self, while desire clings to the sheaths of the Self, the bodies that the Self wears. The separate Self wants to be united with all the other separate Selves. This is love. Being detached from things is called dispassion, and it is a very different thing. Love is the very Self of the Self, so you must protect it. As you try to become less emotional, don't kill love. Love is what keeps us alive, even when we're apart. Every separate Self is drawn to the other Self by it. We are all a part of one great whole. Get rid of desire for the things that cover the Self, but don't get rid of love for the Self, that force that never dies and brings Self to Self. In this big climb up, it's better to suffer from love than to turn away from it and make your heart hard against all ties and claims of care. Go through pain for love, even if it's unpleasant. Love, even if it causes pain. The pain will go away, but the love will keep growing. When you reach the unity of the Self, you'll realise that love is the great force that brings everything together.

There are a lot of people who try to kill love but end up hurting themselves more and becoming less human in the process. Love and caring relationships with other people are how the Self comes out. People say that the Masters love all people as much as a mother loves her eldest child. The love they have for each other isn't watered down to be cool; it's love for all raised to the heat of the highest specific loves of smaller minds. If a teacher tells you to kill love and not care about human feelings, you should never trust that teacher. That's the path that goes to the left.

Meditation With and Without Seed

The next step is how we're going to meditate. What do we mean when we say "mediate"? Every man can't meditate in the same way. The goal is always the same: to calm the mind. However, the method used must be tailored to each person's personality. Let's say you are a man with a strong will, a lot of intelligence, and a love of thinking. Let us say that the only way you've been able to clear your mind is through linked links of thought and argument. Use the knowledge you've already had. Don't think that one attempt will be enough to calm your mind. Don't let your mind stray even a hair's breadth from a reasonable line of thought. Follow it step by step, link by link. Do not let your thoughts wander to other things. Hold it firmly in one line, and stability will come about over time. Then, when your thoughts can no longer go any further and you can see no further, stop. You have reached the highest point of your thinking and the end of your chain of arguments. When you're thinking the most, hold on tight to the last link in the chain. Keep your mind there, steady and very quiet, waiting for whatever may come. You will be able to keep this attitude for a long time after some time.

The way to do something is through devotion, not through reasoning, for someone whose imagination is better than their reasoning. Let him ask his imagination to help him. I think he should picture a scene with the thing he loves as the main character. Then, like a painter making a picture, he should add all the parts of the scene one by one. He has to work at it like a painter works on a canvas: line by line. His brush is his mind. The work will move very slowly at first, but soon the picture will start to show up when called. He would picture the scene over and over, focusing less and less on the things around him and more and more on the central person, who was the idol of his heart. The mind is brought under control and steady by drawing it to a point in this way, and this is done gradually with the imagination. He takes charge of the mind. The man's faith will decide what he will devote himself to. Let's say, like many of you, that his object of love is Sri Krishna. Picture Him in any part of His life on earth, like the battle of Kurukshetra. Imagine both sides' armies ready for war. Picture Arjuna on the floor of the chariot, sad and hopeless. Then, focus on Sri Krishna, the charioteer, friend, and teacher. Then, keep your eyes on the main figure and give your whole heart to Him with love. Place your trust in Him, be still, and wait for what might happen, just like before.

"Meditation with seed" is the name for this. "The seed" refers to the main idea or the last piece of evidence. Through this slow and steady process of halting, you have steadied the wandering mind over time. Finally, you are focused on the core thought or figure and are poised there. Let that go now. Get rid of the main thought, the idea, or the meditation seed. Let go of everything. But keep your mind in the place you've reached, the highest point, and stay strong and alert. To me, this is meditation without a seed. Hold your breath and wait in the void and quiet. Before, you were in the "cloud," and now you're going through the situation that was sketched. There will be a change all of a sudden that will be clear, amazing, and stupefying. As it was said, a voice will be heard in that silence. In that empty space, a Form will show itself. In that empty sky, a Sun will rise, and in its light, you will understand that you are the Sun. You will also know that what seems empty to your senses is full to your Spirit, and what sounds quiet to your senses is full of music to your Spirit.

You can learn to control your mind and train your wandering thoughts in this way, which will lead you to enlightenment. Be careful with this one. While you are meditating with a seed, you can't do this. until you can firmly hold on to your seed for a long time and keep your attention on it the whole time. It's the empty feeling of being ready to act. not the empty feeling of going to sleep soon. If your mind isn't in that state, the fact that it's empty is dangerous. It leads to possession, infatuation, and being able to talk to ghosts. It is only smart to shoot for emptiness after you have trained your mind so well that it can focus on a single point for a long time and stay alert when that point is dropped.

People sometimes ask, "What if I do this and manage to lose consciousness of my body? What if I rise to a higher level? Is it certain that I will return to my body?" Now that I've left the body, am I sure I'll come back?" Men get scared when they think about not coming back. He says that Spirit is everything and matter is nothing, but he still doesn't like to lose touch with his body. When he does, he fears losing touch and falls back to earth after going through all the trouble to leave it. But you shouldn't be afraid of that. All of these things will not change the fact that the record of your past will still be there.

This question is like, "Why should a state of Pralaya ever end and a new state of Manvantara begin?" From a Hindu psychological point of view, the answer is the same: even if you throw away the seed of a thought, you can't get rid of the traces that thought left behind. Each of these traces is a germ, and it tries to draw matter back to itself so that it can express itself again. This mark is known as samskara, which means "no matter." No matter how high you go beyond the real mind, there will always be a trace of what you have thought and known in the thinking principle. This will pull you back. No matter how hard you try, your past will always follow you around until your life is over. This is also what brings a person back to life when their time in heaven is over. It shows how the law of rhythm works. This state is talked about in Light on the Path, a great book on the occult, and the student is shown to be in the silence. The author then says, "A clear voice will come from the peace-filled silence." This voice will say, "It's not good; you've reaped, now you must sow." You will listen because you know this sound is the silence itself.

What does the saying "Thou hast reaped, now thou must sow" mean? The phrase refers to the great rhythmic law that even controls the Logoi and Ishvaras. This is the law of the Mighty Breath, which forces every piece that is split for a while to come back together. A Logos can leave His world, and it will go away when He looks at Himself, because He created space and time.

He could go deep into the infinite depths of being, but He would still be stuck with the samskara of the past world, the vague memory, and the seed of maya. To get away from it would mean turning into Brahma

Nirguna instead of Ishvara. Maya is what Ishvara is, and Ishvara is what maya is. There comes a time, even in pralaya, when the rest is over and the inner life demands to be shown again. This is when the turning outward starts and a new universe appears. This is the law of activity and rest: after doing something, you need to rest, and then you want to do something again. This is how the world and our lives work. Because in the eternal, both rest and action are always there, and in what we call time, they happen one after the other, even though they happen at the same time and all the time in eternity.

Mantra Recitation

Let's see how much we can help ourselves with this tough job. I want to draw your attention to something that will help starters a lot.

Your cars are always moving around. Every vibration in the vehicle causes a change in awareness that goes along with it. Is there a way to stop these vibrations and keep the car steady so that spirit can be still? One way is to say a phrase over and over again. A mantra is a machine that checks sound. You don't use your willpower or your imagination. Instead, you save those skills for other times and use a mantra instead. There is a clear order to the sounds that make up a phrase. The vibrations of the cars become one with each other when those sounds are played over and over again in a rhythmic way. So, you can't translate a phrase because translating changes the sounds. Not only in Hinduism, but also in Buddhism, Roman Catholicism, Islam, and among the Parsis, people use chants. These mantras are never translated because they lose their meaning when the sounds are changed. The words may become a beautiful prayer, but they are not a chant. Even though your translation is inspired and beautiful, it is not a live mantra. It will no longer harmonise the vibrations of the sheaths around it, which will let the mind stop moving. The lyrics and the inspired prayer can be translated in your mind. But a catchphrase is one of a kind and can't be translated. It is true that poetry is wonderful; it can move the mind, please the ear, and be sublime and beautiful, but it is not a mantra.

Awareness

Let's talk about focus. You ask a man if he can handle it. Right away, he says, "Oh, that's hard." I've tried many times and failed." But ask him the same thing but this time in a different way: "Can you pay attention to something?" Right away, he'll say, "Yes, I can do that."

Pay attention by concentrating. Attention that stays on one thing at a time, also called concentration. Your mind will be clear if you pay attention to what you do. A lot of people try to meditate but don't know why they don't get better. How do you think that meditating for thirty minutes and having thoughts all over the place for twenty-three and a half hours during the day and night will help you focus for thirty minutes? "You have undone during the day and night what you did in the morning," Penelope said as she took the web she had made apart. You have to pay attention all the time if you want to become a Yogi. You need to work on focusing every hour that you are awake. Now you think about different things for hours on end and wonder why you don't succeed. It would be amazing if you did. Every day, you need to pay attention to everything you do. That is definitely hard to do. In the beginning, you might find it easier if you pick out a small part of your day's work and give it your full, undivided attention. Don't think about anything else. It doesn't matter what it is. It could be adding up a column of numbers or reading a book. It doesn't matter what. Things that are in front of the mind are not important; how the mind feels about them is. This is the only way to learn how to focus. Centre your attention on the task at hand for now, and put it down when you're done. When you do this regularly for a few months, you'll be surprised at how easy it is to focus your mind. The body will also soon learn to do many things on its own. Once you make something do something regularly, it will start to do it on its own after a while, and then you can do two or three things at once. Women in England, for example, love to knit a lot. When a girl first starts to knit, she has to pay close attention to her fingers. She must keep her eyes on her fingers at all times, or she will make a mistake. One thing she does every day, and now her fingers have learned to focus on the work without her help. She can leave her fingers to knit while she does something else with her mind. You can also train your mind in the same way that the girl trained her fingers. Not only the body, but also the mind can be taught to do something on its own. The last thing is that your greatest consciousness can always stay on the Supreme. The lower consciousness in the body, on the other hand, will do the things of the body perfectly because it has been trained to do them perfectly. This is what you can do with these Yoga lessons.

This kind of practice makes you stronger and better, and it gets you ready to study Yoga more seriously.

Hurdles in Yoga

Before we talk about the skills you need to do this specific practice, let's go over the problems that Patanjali says can get in the way of Yoga.

There are many things that can get in the way of yoga. First, illness: you can't do yoga if you're sick; it requires good health because it puts a lot of strain on your body. Second, a dull mind: you need to be aware and active in your thoughts. When you question, remember that you have to be able to make up your mind. Then carelessness: this is one of the biggest problems with newbies; they read something without paying attention, and they get it wrong. A man who is lazy and doesn't want to work hard can't be a Yogi. How can someone who is inactive and doesn't have the power or will to work hard do what is needed in this line? The next one, having a worldly outlook, is clearly a problem. This is another big problem: having the wrong ideas about things. "Right notion" is one of the most important things you need to do to do yoga. "Right notion" means that the thought goes with the outside truth; that a person must be basically true so that his thought goes with fact; if a person is not true, he cannot do yoga. Not getting the point, being stupid, irrational, making the important seem less important, and the other way around. Finally, instability is something that can't be a yogi because it makes yoga useless. Even a little instability makes yoga pointless.

Skills in Yoga

Is Yoga open to everyone? No. But anyone with a good education can get ready to use it in the future. As with anything else, you need special skills to make quick progress. In any of the sciences, a person can learn without having special skills, but they can't become experts in that field. The same is true for Yoga. Anyone with a fair amount of ability can learn something useful from yoga and use it, but they can't expect to be good at yoga in this life unless they start with certain skills. That is the right thing to say, because if any special science needs certain skills to be successful, then the study of sciences can't be less demanding on its students than the other sciences.

"Can I become a great mathematician?" someone asked me. What do I need to say? You have to be naturally good at maths if you want to be a great scientist. You can't be a great thinker in this life if you don't have that skill. Yes, this does mean you can't learn maths, though. You have to be born with a special ability for maths to be a great mathematician. If you are born with a certain skill, it means you have practiced it many times before and now it is ready to use. The same goes for Yoga. It's something that every man can learn. But to be a great Yogi, you have to practise all your life. If these things are behind you, you will have been born with the right skills in this birth.

In order to be good at Yoga, you need to have three qualities. The first is a strong need. "Desire deeply." You need this kind of desire to break the strong bonds of desire that hold you to the outside world. Also, you will never get through all the problems that come your way without that strong drive. You have to believe that you will win in the end and be determined to keep going until you do. The desire must be so strong and strong-rooted that problems only make it stronger. For this kind of man, a problem is like adding fuel to a fire. It burns even more strongly as it grabs on to it and finds fuel for the fire. To the yogi, problems and challenges are just fuel for the fire of their strong desire. He only becomes more set in his ways because he faces problems.

Don't have this strong desire? That means you're new to the work, but you can start getting ready for it in this life. You can make desire happen through thought, but not through desire itself. You can't train your desire nature from the desire nature itself.

What is it about us that makes us want something? Memory and fantasy are the two things that make you want something the most when you look inside your own mind. Because of this, thought is the way that all changes in desire can happen. The only thing that can make you creative is your thought, or imagination. It is through imagination that your skills will be revealed. When you think about something you want, the desire for it gets stronger. If you want to want Yoga, then think of it as something you want. If you think about what yoga does for people and what it means for the world when you become a yogi, your desire will grow. Because you can only control your desire through thought. It doesn't do anything on its own. Either you want the thing or you don't want it, and you can't do anything about it within the limits of your desire. As was already said, you can't change your desire with another desire. Go to a different part of yourself called thought. In thought, you can make yourself want or not want anything you want, as long as you use the right techniques, which are actually pretty easy to do. What is it that you want to own something? To feel better, because you believe it. You may know from past experience that it does not make you happy in the long run, but instead brings you sadness, trouble, and stress. The way to get rid of that wish is right in front of you. Think about what will happen in the end. Think about all the terrible things for a long time. Skip over the short-term pleasure and keep your mind on the pain that comes after your desire is satisfied. Once you've done that for about a month, the sight of those things you want will turn you off. Because you will have linked it to pain in your mind, you will naturally avoid it. You won't want it. You changed what people want by using your ideas. Visualising the worst things that will happen if you give in to a vice is the most powerful way to break it. If you want to get a young man who is prone to wastefulness to think of an old wasteful person, show him that person as worn out and wanting something without being able to get it. If you can get him to think that way, he will start to shy away from what was appealing to him before; the man will be afraid to hold on to what he wants because it is so ugly. And the person who wants to become a yogi has to use his mind to figure out which desires he will give in to and which he will kill.

A strong will comes after a strong wish. Will is wanting something changed, its direction changes from outside to inside. You need to make your will stronger if it's weak. As with other weak things, you should work on making it stronger by using it. If a boy knows that his arms are weak, he will say, "My arms are weak, but I will do gymnastics and work on the parallel bars. That way, my arms will get stronger." The will is the same way. Putting your little, weak will to use will make it stronger.

Say something like, "I'm going to do this every morning," and then follow through. A weak will can handle one thing at a time. If you tell yourself you'll do something at a certain time, you will soon feel bad about breaking your word. You should keep this word to yourself for at least one day. Then for one week, then for two weeks. Once you've done something easy, you can move on to something harder, and so on. By making people do something, you build their will. With each passing day, it gets stronger, and you feel stronger inside. First, you need to really want it. After that, change it into a strong will.

The third thing you need to do to do yoga is to be smart in many areas. You can't manage your mind if you don't have one to manage. So, you need to improve your mind. You need to study. I don't mean reading books when I say "study." I mean to think. There's a chance that your mind will still be weak after reading a dozen books. But if you've read one important book the right way, reading slowly and thinking a lot will make you smarter and your mind stronger.

These are the things you want: a strong drive, a strong will, and a sharp mind. Those are the skills you need to develop in order to be able to practise Yoga. If your mind is as shaky as a child's or like a butterfly, you need to make it steady. You have to study and think about that a lot. You need to open up the mind you'll be using.

Going Forth and Coming Back

It will help you do this and change your wish if you understand that humanity's great evolution has two paths: the Path of Forthgoing and the Path of Return.

Needs and wants are important and helpful on the Path, or marga, of Pravritti, which is where most people are now. Men will evolve faster if they have more desire along that path. These are the things that make people do things. Without these, the stagnates, he does nothing. If Isvara didn't want desire to be a part of development, why would He have filled the worlds with things that people would want? He treats people like a smart mother treats her child: with care. She doesn't teach the child on the benefits of walking or help it understand how the muscles in its legs work. She holds out a shiny, bright toy and tells the child, "Come get it." When the child's desire comes back, it starts to crawl, which helps it learn to walk. He has placed toys around us so that they are just out of reach, and He says, "Come, kids, take these." Come get love, money, fame, and respect from other people. Walk and put in some work for them." Also, just like kids, we work very hard and fight to get these toys. The toy breaks into pieces when we grab it, so it's useless. Those who are wealthy fight, suffer, and work hard to get it, and then they ask, "How shall we spend this wealth?" There was an American millionaire I read about who was going from city to city to give away his huge amount of money. He learned from his mistake. That man will never, ever be tempted to work hard for the toy of wealth again. Men work harder than anyone else because they want fame and power. But when you grab them and hold them in your hand, you get tired. The great politician, the boss of the country, the man that millions of people look up to: follow him home, and you will see how power wears you down and how passion dies. So, does God make fun of us with all the things? No. The goal has been to bring out the power of the Self in order to improve man's innate abilities. The outcome of the great lila can be seen in the growth of human faculties. That's how we learn to bring out the God in us; that's what happens when the divine Father plays with His children.

But kids lose their desire for things too soon, and they only learn half of what they need to learn. That's one of the problems in India right now. You have a powerful spiritual belief that came naturally to the souls that were born years ago. They were ready to give up the fruit of their labour and work for the Supreme to do what He wanted.

But India needs to wake up its desire right now. It might look like going back, but it's really moving forward. While the theory is true, it was meant for older souls who were ready for it. The younger souls who are now being born into the people are not ready for it. They say it over and over again, as if it were a hypnotic spell. They become lazy because they don't want anything badly enough to make them work hard. Because of this, the country as a whole is getting worse. People have forgotten the old lesson that different things should be presented to souls of different ages. Now, everyone is supposed to be looking for ideal perfection, which can only be reached after the first steps have been successfully completed. The same thing happens with the "Sermon on the Mount" in Christian countries, but people there give in to it and don't think about it. There is no country that tries to follow the "Sermon on the

Mount." Not just any men or women can use it; only saints can. People who are on the Path of Forthgoing need to want to move forward.

What does the Path of Nivritti look like? It's the Way Back. That wish has to end, and the Self-determined will has to take its place. When someone starts on the Path of Return, the last thing they want is to work with the Supreme Will. They align their will with the Supreme Will, give up all their other goals, and work to turn the wheel of life as long as the law of life says they have to. Want on the Path of Going Out turns into will on the Path of Coming Back; the soul works with the law in agreement with God. When you're on the Path of Forthgoing, your thoughts are always on, moving around, and changing. When you're on the Path of Return, they turn into reason. Reason holds the lower mind down and guides the bull. On the Path of Forthgoing, work and activity are wild things that hold the average person back. On the Path of Return, work turns into sacrifice, which breaks its hold on the person. So, these are the ways that three parts show up, as shown on the Paths of Going Out and Coming Back.

When happiness shows up as desire, it changes into will. When wisdom shows up as a thought, it changes into reason. What started out as work turns into sacrifice.

"Why is will placed in the human being as the correspondence of bliss in the Divine?" is a question that comes up a lot. Consciousness (chit), happiness (ananda), and existence (sat) are the three most important traits of God. And now it's very clear that awareness is like intelligence in people—it's the same thing, but smaller. It is also clear that existence and action go hand in hand. You are only real when you act in the world. Just the way the word is formed—"ex, out of"—shows that it is life. This leaves the third, happiness, to connect with will. This makes some people curious, so they ask, "What is the connection between bliss and will?" But if you think about what you want and why you want it, you can figure out the puzzle. The Self is happiness itself. If you drop that nature into matter, what will the happy nature look like? The desire for happiness, the pursuit of desirable things that it thinks will give it the happiness that is inherent in it and that it is always trying to achieve despite the challenges of the world. Because it is bliss, it wants to be happy, and that wish to be happy needs to be turned into will. Anytime you look into these connections, they all mean something very important. That common "will-to-live" turns into the "desire for happiness" that you find in every person and every living thing. You think that happiness is your right, you hate being unhappy, and you wonder what you did wrong to earn it. Has it ever occurred to you that this is a very accurate description of who you are? You don't ask the same thing about happy, even though that's just how you are. No, it's not happiness that needs to be explained. It's pain, things that go against the nature of the Self, which is bliss. Taking this into account, we can see that both desire and will are what make us want to be happy. But one is unaware and is pulled out by things in the outside world, while the other is self-aware and is led and controlled from within. When the same thing rules from the inside, it's called will, and it comes from the outside. They are not different in any way. So, desire on the Path of Going Away turns into will on the Path of Coming Back.

When man changes his want, thought, and work into will, reason, and sacrifice, he is moving closer to God and living by giving up things.

A man goes through a strange change when he has really given up. You have to fight for everything you want on the Path of Forthgoing. On the Path of Return, nature gives you all of her gifts. When a person stops wanting things, all treasures fall on them, because they are now a conduit through which all good things move to those around them. Give up trying to get what you want and look for the good. Then everything will be yours. Stop asking for your own small water tank to be filled, and you will turn into a pipe connected to the live source of all waters, the source that never runs out and the waters that always come up. Giving up something means having the power to keep working for the good of everyone. This work can't fail because it is done by the Supreme Worker through His worker.

If you are doing a real act of kindness and don't get any money for it, what does that mean? It means you haven't learned how to really give up something yet. Since you're holding on to what you can see and what you can do, the wealth doesn't flow through your hands.

Purification of the Physical and Spiritual Bodies

The unfolding of powers belongs to the side of consciousness; purification of bodies belongs to the side of matter. You must purify each of your three working bodies--mental, astral and physical. Without that purification you had better leave yoga alone. First of all, how shall you purify the thought body? By right thinking. Then you must use imagination, your great creative tool, once more. Imagine things, and, imagining them, you will form your thought-body into the organisation that you desire. Imagine something strongly, as the painter imagines when he is going to paint. Visualise an object if you have the power of visualisation at all: if you have not, try to make it. It is an artistic faculty, of course, hut most people have it more or less. See how far you can reproduce perfectly a face you see daily. By such practice you will be strengthening your imagination, and by strengthening your imagination you will be making the great tool with which you have to practice in Yoga.

There is another use of the imagination which is very valuable. If you will imagine in your thought-body the presence of the qualities that you desire to have, and the absence of those which you desire not to have, you are half-way to having and not having them. Also, many of the troubles of your life might be weakened if you would imagine them on right lines before you have to go through them. Why do you wait helplessly until you meet them in the physical world. If you thought of your coming trouble in the morning, and thought of yourself as acting perfectly in the midst of it (you should never scruple to imagine yourself perfect), when the thing turned up in the day, it would have lost its power, and you would no longer feel the sting to the same extent. Now each of you must have in your life something that troubles you. Think of yourself as facing that trouble and not minding it, and when it comes, you will be what you have been thinking. You might get rid of half your troubles and your faults, if you would deal with them through your imagination.

As the thought body, becomes purified in this way, you must turn to the astral body. The astral body is purified by right desire. Desire nobly, and the astral body will evolve the organs of good desires instead of the organs of evil ones. The secret of all progress is to think and desire the highest, never dwelling on the fault, the weakness, the error, but always on the perfected power, and slowly in that way you will be able to build up perfection in yourself. Think and desire, then, in order to purify the thought body and the astral body.

And how shall you purify the physical body? You must regulate it in all its activities--in sleep, in food, in exercise, in everything. You cannot have a pure physical body with impure mental and astral bodies so that the work of imagination helps also in the purification of the physical. But you must also regulate the physical body in all its activities. Take for instance, food. The Indian says truly that every sort of food has a dominant quality in it, either rhythm, or activity, or inertia, and that all foods fall under one of these heads. Now the man who is to be a yogi must not touch any food which is on the way to decay. Those things belong to the tamasic foods--all foods, for instance, of the nature of game, of venison, all food which is showing signs of decay (all alcohol is a product of decay), are to be avoided. Flesh foods come under the quality of activity. All flesh foods are really stimulants. All forms in the animal kingdom are built up to express animal desires and animal activities. The yogi cannot afford to use these in a body meant for the higher processes of thought. Vitality, yes, they will give that; strength, which does not last, they will give that; a sudden spurs of energy, yes, meat will give that; but those are not the things which the yogi wants; so he puts aside all those foods as not available for the work he desires, and chooses his food out of the most highly vitalised products. All the foods which tend to growth, those are the most highly vitalised, grain, out of which the new plant will grow, is packed full of the most nutritious substances; fruits; all those things which have growth as their next stage in the life cycle, those are the rhythmic foods, full of life, and building up a body sensitive and strong at the same time.

Boundary Watchers

There are many kinds of these. First, the elements. They try to stop people from getting to the astral plane. This makes sense, since the Rupa Devas are form-elementals who are in charge of building up the lower countries. Because people are destructive, the Rupa Devas hate them very much. That's why they don't like him at all. Everywhere he goes, he ruins their work, walks on plants, and kills animals. As a result, the whole world of nature hates the name of man. They work together to stop the person who is just becoming aware of the astral plane for the first time and try to scare him because they think he will bring bad things into the new world. If you don't mind them, they can't do anything. When the man entering the astral plane is hit by that rush of elemental force, he must stay quiet and not care. He must take the stance, "I am a higher product of evolution than you are; you can't hurt me." Peace, I am your friend, not your enemy!" It's possible for him to get through the big wave of elemental force if he is strong enough to stand there. A lot of the fears that some people have at night that don't seem to have a reason are caused by this hatred. You are more in tune with the astral plane at night than during the day, and the things that live there don't like people as much. But once the elementals see that you are not harmful or a wretched thing, they become just as friendly towards you as they were before. That's the first shape of the person who lives on the doorway. Again, this is why it's important to eat clean, rhythmic food. If you eat meat and drink booze, you will attract lower elementals that enjoy the smell of blood and spirits, and they will make it impossible for you to see and understand clearly. They will rush around you, push their thoughts on you, and leave their marks on your astral body. This will create a shell of unwanted people hanging off of your aura, making it hard for you to see and hear clearly. In order to teach Yoga on the right road, this is the main reason why people should never eat meat or drink alcohol.

The second type of dweller on the brink is our own past thoughts. These shapes, which come from the bad lives we've lived in the past and are thought forms of all kinds of evil, are what we see when we first connect with the astral plane. They belong to us but look like outside shapes or objects, and they try to scare away their creator. You can only beat them by telling them in a firm voice, "You are not mine anymore; you belong to my past, not my present." I'm not going to give you any of my life." In this way, you will slowly wear them down until they are completely gone. Astral travel for the first time can be very hard, and this is one of the hardest things that people have to deal with. Obviously, if a person has been exposed to stronger, more negative thought forms, like those that come from black magic, this form of the dweller will be much stronger and more dangerous. The struggle between the neophyte and these dwellers from his past, who are backed by the masters of the black side, is often very desperate.

Now we'll talk about one of the scariest types of people who live on the brink. Imagine a man who, in the past, has slowly identified with the lower part of his nature and fought against the higher. He has done this by paralysing himself, using his higher powers for lower goals, and lowering his mind so that it is only a slave to his lower desires. He goes through an interesting change. The life that belongs to the Ego in him is taken up by the body and mixed with the lower lives that makeup the body. Instead of helping the Spirit, it is pulled away to help the lower and becomes part of the animal life of the lower bodies. This makes the Ego and his higher bodies weaker while the animal life of the lower bodies gets stronger. When things are like this, the Ego will sometimes get so sick of his cars that when death takes away his body, he will throw the others away completely. He will even leave the desecrated temple from time to time while he is still alive. When this happens, the man usually reincarnates very quickly because he has already torn himself away from his astral and mental bodies and doesn't have any bodies to live in the astral and mental worlds. He has to quickly make new bodies and come back to this world to restart. The old astral and mental bodies don't break down when the new astral and mental bodies are formed and born into the world. Instead, the affinity between the old and new arises because they both had the same owner, the same tenant. The highly vitalized old astral and mental bodies will attach themselves to the new astral and mental bodies and become the most terrifying form of the dweller on the threshold.

The dweller can take on these different forms, and all of them are talked about in books about these topics. However, I don't think you will find a clear description like the one above in a single book. Along with these, there are also the direct attacks of the Dark Brothers, which come in many shapes and sizes. The most common shape they take is the form of a yogi's over-the-top virtue. The yogi is not attacked by his flaws, but by his strengths, because a strength that is too great can turn into a weakness. Sometimes the worst things are at the edges; the golden mean is the good thing. So, values turn into tempters in the rough parts of the mental and astral worlds, and the Brothers of the Shadow use them to catch people who aren't paying attention.

The four normal ordeals on the spiritual plane are caused by earth, water, fire, and air. I'm not talking about those here. These are small problems that don't even come up when talking about these bigger problems. Without a doubt, you need to learn that you are in charge of all astral matter and that earth, water, and other things can't hurt you. To use a figure of speech, those are pretty simple rules. People who are part of a Masonic body will know these trials as parts of the language they use in their rituals.

There is also one more risk. You could hurt yourself by repercussion. If you are faced with a physical danger on the astral plane and are foolish enough to think it can hurt you, it will hurt your physical body. You could get a cut, a bruise, or something else during a mental journey. This is how I embarrassed myself once. While I was busy with something else, I noticed that the ship's mast was about to fall. For some reason, I forgot about it for a moment and thought, "That mast will fall on me." That thought came true, because when I woke up in the morning, I had a big bruise where the mast had hit me. People often think the same things until you fix the problem with their mind. Their mind automatically thinks the things it is used to thinking down here.

You can protect yourself in one way as you become more sensitive. Be completely honest in what you think, what you say, and what you do. In the greater world, every thought and wish comes true. You are making a lot of scary and false forms if you don't care about the truth here. If you think truth, speak truth, and live truth, you will be free from the spirit world's lies.

Preparation for Yoga

Some people say that I set the bar so high for teaching that no one can ever hope to reach it. That being said, I haven't said that no one can become a disciple if they don't match the perfect disciple. One can. We do it anyway, but it's dangerous. In one area, a man may be very skilled, but in another, he may have a major flaw. He can still become a student even though he made a big mistake, but he will have to suffer because of it. As an initiate, the price he has to pay for his mistakes is ten times what it would have been as a normal person. That's why I set the bar so high. I never said that someone had to completely reach the ideal before they could become a student. What I did say was that there are huge risks if someone doesn't meet these requirements. People who have seen what happens when people with character flaws go through the doorway should point out that these flaws should be fixed first. On the other side, every flaw you bring through the doorway turns into a knife that will stab you. To avoid this, you should clean up as much as you can before you are advanced enough in any area to say, "I will pass through that gateway." I meant for that to be understood when I talked about what it takes to be a follower. I have been on the old path that says a disciple should bring these things with them. If he does not, Jesus' words are true: he will be beaten with many stripes. This is because people can do things in the outside world that won't hurt them much, but they will hurt them very badly when they are on the Path.

The End

What will be the end of this long fight? What is the point of going up? What is the prize for the big battle? What does the yogi finally get to? He comes together. There are times when I doubt that a lot of people would really want to reach union if they knew what it meant. When you reach equality, many of the "virtues" that you have in your everyday life will go away. When the sense of togetherness starts to show, many of the things you admire will no longer help but hurt. When unity is reached, none of the traits that are useful in everyday life can exist. This includes moral outrage, aversion to evil, and judging others. If you feel like evil is pulling you away, it means that your Higher Self is starting to awaken and see how dangerous evil is. He pulls your body away from it forcibly. You can start living a decent life after that. It's better to hate evil at that point than to not care about it. It's an important step. When a person realises unity, or sees God in himself, he can't feel any of those things. Being united means not being able to judge another person. "I do not judge anyone," the Christ said. He can't be turned off by anyone. The criminal is himself; how can he be turned away from himself? He doesn't have a "I" or a "Thee," because we are all one.

A lot of people really don't want this to happen. It's not something that many people really want. The person who has reached unity doesn't see any difference between himself and the worst person in the world. His only sight is the God who walks in the sinner. He knows that the sin is not in the God, but in the skin. There is only that one change. Someone who knows the true greatness of the Self never judges another person because they see them as themselves and themselves as others. This is unity. A lot of us talk about unity, but how many of us really live it? And that's not even what the yogi wants. Being one with the Self is more important than being a brother. Brotherhood will reach its peak in the Sixth Root Race. The Seventh Root Race will know who they are and understand how one the human race is. Catching a glimpse of the beauty of that high idea, the greatness of the unity where "I" and "mine" and "you" and "yours" have disappeared and where we are all one life, elevates nature towards divinity. Those who can see that unity are fair; they are closer to realising the beauty that is God.

Chapter 5
Mindfulness

Having concentration means being in the middle (con and centrum). Bringing the mind to a single point is what it means when used to describe thinking. Every person needs to learn focusing on their own thoughts and feelings. In other words, every person tries to focus on a place inside and outside of his own world with a degree of accuracy. Concentration "without" is shown when you focus on Nature the whole time, like when you're learning a business, trade, job, science, art, or trade. This is Evolution, mental force that makes you want to help others. This is what I'm going to call Objective Concentration. "Within" concentration means taking your mind off of the outside world and focusing on "God," "Spirit," "Heaven," "Religion," "Peace," "Nirvana," "Eternity," and other ideas. This is involution, which means coming in or bad energy.

Objective Concentration practice alone will turn you into a tough, useful man of the world or a great businessman. You are smart and sharp. You don't think much about the world. You can only think of making money, having fun, and taking care of business matters. You're a "worldling of the world," which means you're smart, wealthy, and good at what you do. In terms of your mental life, though, you're as stupid as a child. "Deeply immersed in matter and literally made of dust," this is the Objective Mind. "It is the mind of common sense, wisdom, prudence, methodical arrangement, order, discipline, classification, and the skill and knowledge of a specialist in any field of art or science." Scientists, mathematicians, businesspeople, and other smart people use this part of their minds a lot. When the Subjective Mind isn't in charge, it can only see differences and variety. It is Maya's slave and kills the Real.

Subjective Concentration means looking inside yourself for the Kingdom of Heaven. "God is Spirit, and those who worship Him must worship in Spirit and Truth." The great scientist LAPLACE said that he had looked through his telescope at the sky and not found God or Heaven. Oh, poor LAPLACE! He did not look for God based on his own feelings, but on facts.

Seeing the Kingdom of God doesn't happen, it's "within" you. Focusing on the present moment is the most important thing in religion. The human body has to use up energy and eventually die in order to do objective work, since all objective concentration means "going from" the Absolute centre, which is God, and this uses up Spiritual Energy. Subjective Concentration means "coming to" the heart, so it keeps this energy alive and makes it stronger. Nature now moves to and from us, and Spirit is the centre of life. This two-way action is called polarity, and it can be described as either evolution or involution, which means negative or positive. Life gets involved, or "wrapped up," in form at the negative pole. Life "evolves" or shows itself in nature at the positive end. In Subjective Concentration, you go back to the Absolute Will, which is an endless source of power, to get more supplies. Jesus was able to rule the outside world by raising the dead and healing the sick because his pure soul could only receive good things from God and give good things to the outside world. God is the source of all power. I want to stress how important it is to be magnetically passive towards the Universal Will and then calm and positive towards the phenomenal world, which is a projection of the lower nature and needs to be dealt with masterfully, without fear, and with confidence. Be upbeat about the outside world. Be negative and open to the Will-force of the Lord. Do not forget this. Today I want to talk about the most important and strong truth in the Science of prayer. A mind that is praying lets a huge amount of Divine Energy flow into it just by having faith and expecting the best. Near the centre of all power, knowledge, and love, it drinks deeply of the living waters of life, to the point where even the face or flesh starts to shine through prayer because of this self-polarization, if I may use that word. This is the reason why a prayer will always get an answer. Remember what Lord Rosebery said about Oliver Cromwell, the great Puritan mystic? If not, let me quote: "His huge success came from the fact that he was a practical mystic—the scariest and most dangerous combination of traits possible." The person who combines inspiration that seems to come from close contact with the supernatural and the celestial, along with the energy of a strong man of action, is one who lives in communion on his own Sinai and, when he chooses to come down to this world, seems armed with nothing less than the terrors and decrees of the Almighty Himself. At this point, both types of focus need to be used to keep the two poles in a state of balanced growth.

You will do the daily work that you are naturally good at in the common good (Objective Concentration). When you are done with your daily job, you will regularly practise Subjective Concentration to return to the embrace of the Universal Spirit.

Now you will reach the goal of peace in the middle of the day's work and sweat.

To learn about the rules of the outside world, you need to be able to accurately observe it. To understand any field of science, you must focus your attention and push objective concentration to its highest level, which is perfect knowledge or illumination.

Pratyahara and Dharana are the steps that come before Objective Concentration. For example, think about a scientist. He knows that thought force is spread out when the mind is busy with many things. He is too smart to be a leader, a musician, etc., and a great scientist at the same time. He slowly pulls his attention away from everything else and stops on one subject or a group of subjects.

Pratyahara is the mind's ongoing work to separate itself in this way.

When this effort finally works and the mind stays steady and focused, you have reached dharana. This steadiness goes further with dhyana. From Dhyana on, the student can't learn anything else from books. His thoughts are on new experiments and study, and what he knows becomes clearer and clearer. By going on and on about the same thing over and over, you learn everything there is to know about the subject. This is Samadhi's true point of view. When these steps are all done, they make up one Samayana. There is something about Samadhi that you can't learn from books or papers. You will understand these things better as you learn more about Yoga and your Soul-Vision. That thing will come to you if you do what I say next. Do not be sad.

Maya

First, what is Maya, which means "ignorance of the real"? Look at the face of a watch. You already know that the machinery behind the watch controls the hands. Both are important. If you think that the watch's hands move on their own, you are not smart. This world we can see is the dial-plate of the invisible. Ignorance, or maya, keeps you from seeing this truth. That is, having objective knowledge keeps you from seeing the subjective side of life, and you can only see the material world. But you don't need to be afraid of that danger because you know both factual and subjective. Focusing on the objective mind over the emotional is a dangerous thing to do. Do both to complete yourself. However, the subjective should always come first, last, and be the light of the objective. Also, keep this in mind: if your mind is connected to the objective world in any way, try your hardest to separate it and focus on the subjective side of life. If you don't, you will cause yourself unimaginable pain. When a man who is half-spiritual and half-human wants to live a spiritually sensual life, the laws and forces of the two planes of being finally clash. It hurts so much that he can't close his eyes. Finally, cries of pain, sickness, and loss force him to do so. You should know what the world is like, but you shouldn't let its small thoughts, things, and ways connect you to your soul.

Ways to Concentrate Objectively

I. In all undertakings whether of small or great importance shut off all thoughts and ideas except such as have any immediate and direct bearing upon the thing in hand. Pay attention. Bend all the energies of your mind and will upon it till it is completed to your satisfaction. Divert your attention from one thing to another only when you sanction by a resolve and understand why you do so. Your daily work which you must choose according to the special bent of your mind, will present you opportunities.

II. Control impulse. Suppose an idea enters your mind. Compose yourself quietly before carrying out its purport. Consider it. Turn it over in your mind. Contemplate it. Weave your mental energies around it, as it were, till at last the idea with your final decision stands out clear-cut and well-defined. Then proceed to act it out physically with your mental concentration cutting a way for you straight on to the execution of your designing. This is forethought.

III. In perfect concentration time vanishes. In working out a design on which you have set your heart dispense altogether with the element of time and work at it concentratedly for days, months and years with confident expectation of success.

IV. Take a picture, representing a landscape, the interior of a building, an assembly of persons, a square, a triangle or a more complicated geometrical figure. Look at it well. Then lay it aside. Close your eyes. Reproduce the picture mentally in detail. Then repose your mind on the same image to the exclusion of all other thoughts. This is a more fixed and meditative method and will sharpen the mind wonderfully. It will also develop the power of conscious Mental Imagery. The key to Objective Concentration is Conscious Attention, remember.

Active and Inactive Mental Processes

These words suggest two different and distinct ways that the mind works. The active function is what does the free, voluntary thinking. It means putting your mind on a problem that you are aware of. Active meditation means getting rid of all thoughts and ideas that aren't related to what you're studying. Men who are awake and active use this function when they are busy and full of energy. This is the key to building strong willpower and a sharp mind. When you use this tool, you are aware of how hard it is. Conscious attention means focusing your thoughts closely, and you can only do that by using your Will-Power consciously. After a lot of this kind of work, your mind gets tired and begs to rest. One thing you think about, study, or observe should be able to get your full attention. Then you should be able to switch your mind to something else whenever you want. You can train your mind to "give" full attention to any subject you want and then "turn off" all attention to that topic. The mind is restless and jumps from one thing to another. It gets tired of being watched all the time, like a spoiled child. But you need to use Will-Exercise to stop this urge. "Working out builds strength. Practice makes perfect." You need to remember this and train your mind to "pay attention" where it should and not where it shouldn't by being patient and persistent. At first, this kind of restraint will make your mind fight like a horse that has never been tamed. But really, mind-control is the key to all success. Remember that active mentation means focusing on something consciously and on purpose. Passive mentation is thought that happens automatically and without effort. The subconscious or "habit" mind is part of this. When you have a certain thought-groove, energy moves into it without you having to do anything. Passive mentation is what this is. It happens automatically in the mind. Here is an example. Some boys in school find it easy to learn maths, science, and geography right away. It's easy for them to feel sorry for the maths teacher. However, they hate history and language. There are others who just can't "get interested" in maths, but they are great at language, recitation, composition, and history. To be honest, neither of these kids is better than the other. They are all great in their own way. There are examples of natural mentation in math, science, and geography in one set, and examples of it in literature and art in the other. But let's say the first group tried to learn literature and art, and the second group struggled with maths and science. Then both groups would be practicing real concentration. Both sides would work on their willpower and the main function would be used in each set. Can you see? Occultists say that all strength comes from constantly using active mentation and that all weakness comes from this habit of wasting time, focusing on other things, and not paying attention, which is an extension of passive mentation into useless thought-force channels. Being aware of something makes your mind focus and even specialise, just like sunglasses focus and boost the heat from the sun. You will get great results if you put all of your attention on the thing that needs to be done and are really interested in getting it done. If a person has developed and focused concentration power, they hold the key to success. All of their actions, whether they want to or not, will lead them to achieve their goal. So, remember this in the end:

I. Concentration is perfect attention consciously directed to a given point of achievement either objectively or subjectively.

II. Concentration is consecration.

"What ever you do, do it with all your might. Do one thing at a time and do it well." By concentration is meant the directing of all your energies along a special line of achievement. For instance, if you would be a perfect Yogi, you must concentrate, concentrate, morning, noon and night, at all times, along that line of endeavour. You must study all the vast literature on Yoga, Psychology, Metaphysics, Mentalism, etc., and form your own synthesis on same. You must think hard and work hard for Yoga. "Genius is the power to bear infinite pain." Nothing ought to be too great a sacrifice, including your own life, for the right understanding and achievement of Yoga.

All half-heartedness, all insincerity, weakens your nature, and weakness has no place either in heaven or in hell. For the half-hearted man is a traitor unto the Divine within him and must pay dearly for his treachery.

Subjective Concentration

This is a very broad field. You will become stronger than most people if you follow my advice on Thought-Control, Will-Culture, and the Meditation Exercise I'm about to give you with all your heart. But you still need to study and think deeply for yourself before even these can help you in a big way. Don't forget that you are the only one who can teach yourself through insight. Intuition is like getting help from inside. Follow the general rules I give you to the letter, and your Inner Soul Vision, which includes all forms of intuition, will come to life.

a. What is Thought-Force?

"Thoughts are real." Thought is a moving force. Eating food is good for your body, and having good thoughts and feelings is good for your mind. Matter is just a bunch of thought-force or mind-substance thrown together. Everything in the world can be seen objectively. In terms of space, this is huge. "What a man thinks in his heart, that is what he is" applies to each person. There is no doubt about it. Your body is just a form of your thoughts. You can change the way you think and make it fit high goals. So you will always, happily, and right away be in charge of your future. In charge of your own thoughts, you can be in charge of every other man's thoughts too. Your thoughts should always sound high. Your higher life is now available to you. You just need to change the way you think and feel. I'm going to give you some ideas on the same. Please pay attention.

b. Thought-Forms

Thought-Forms and Thought-Waves of different strengths are sent out by each of us based on what we think, feel, and want. Once this force is set in motion, it stays in Ether for a longer or shorter amount of time. It is thought that Thought-Force is a high-level vibrational energy that is concentrated in the Akasa (universal ether). The ether, as you know, fills all space and all matter, from atoms to the sun and stars. Light waves from a star continue to move around hundreds of years after the star itself has died, and heat waves stay in a room even after the source of the heat has been taken away. In the same way, mental energy and the Thought Forms that go with it stay in the ether even after the source of the energy has been taken away.

c. Thought-Atmosphere

In this way, homes, towns, temples, and other places have their own unique Thought-Atmospheres that are created by the people who live there and affect everyone who lives or visits them. There are positive Thought-Atmospheres that inspire, cleanse, and raise, and there are also negative Thought-Atmospheres that weaken, are evil, and are morbid.

The smaller and stronger the vibrations of the energy coming from you, the higher and loftier your general thought-activity tone is. The rate of shaking is based on the quality of the thought. As an example, pictures have been taken through highly sensitive plates, which show what kind of energy was created. From prayer and reverence, pictures were taken of bright, flashing tongues of golden-yellow flame. Rising passion for a good cause led to the formation of rotary shapes that spread out in ever-widening circles of intense power. Forms that were dark, murky, and cloudy came from things like fear, morbidity, worry, and so on.

d. The Human Aura

In the same way, every living thing has a "Aura" of Thought-Force around it that has its own unique rate of vibration, colour forms, etc. Our bodily, mental, and spiritual energies all come together to form this "Aura."

The Adductive Power of Thought

As you think, the quality of your thoughts and feelings creates a magnetic centre in your aura. Vortices are then created, drawing similar types of thought and mental energy to you and combining them with other similar types of energy. This energy then reacts to you and your situation and also has an effect on anyone else who comes within its area, radius, or field of force. That's why "I can," "I will," and "I dare" thoughts bring similar ones to you. This keeps adding to your stock and also inspires and energises everyone else around the world who is buzzing in the same key. So, you can see that we owe it to ourselves and to everyone else to think only good, loving, and high thoughts. Just get ready and send out bold "I can and I will" thoughts into the world's vast pool of thought forces. You will be amazed at how much power you have to influence others and give them energy.

Thought-Control

These four types of thoughts are ruining the lives of almost everyone on Earth. These are them: (2) Thoughts of hate, (3) Thoughts of pleasure, and (4) Thoughts of self-interest. Worry, doubt, shyness, low self-esteem, anger, spite, venom, envy, slander, and other negative emotions that are dirty, mean, weakening the will, bad for health, leading to poverty, and killing the soul come from one or all of these four. You need to cut them off at the roots and finish them off. In your work, make sure you carefully follow these four rules. Only they can give you full power over your thoughts. They are always right:

I. You can break up old thought-habits and build up new ones by sheer force of Will.

II. You can easily become great by associating with some strong-willed, holy, wisdom-steeped soul. This is absolutely necessary and means the finding of your Guru.

III. By auto-suggestion, i.e., by impressing upon your passive mind the particular change you would have it work out.

IV. By thought-absorption, i.e., by constant meditation on that one line of thinking.

Now let me give you a few valuable hints on the above four in detail:

I. & III. Character Building

To get this effect, you can tense your will and make the active part of your mind stronger. This will let the active part "step in" and tell the passive part to drop the old thought habit and pick up the new one. It takes a lot of strength to pull off this amazing trick. When you combine this with auto-suggestion, you can get good results. Focus on your mind that is not doing anything and tell it what to do. Tell your mind in a sincere, sure, and skilled way, "You, my mind, I want you to be fearless, pure, loving, and selfless!" Picture yourself as if you were already these things, and tell your mind again what you want it to do. Do this in silence and all the time, and don't miss a chance to show these qualities in action. At first, your mind will fight you, but if "you" keep up your efforts firmly and determinedly and take advantage of all the chances to "act out" your will, your mind will eventually accept your suggestion and do the same naturally as a habit. Some of you will go out of your way to "act out" a thought once you know that the easiest and most certain way to stop and completely "destroy" a thought-habit is to refuse to let it show up in action. On the other hand, to "create" a new thought-habit, all you have to do is "express" it in action on purpose, which will make it strong for good. You should also strive for "thoroughness" and avoid giving in to your lower nature at all costs. Virginity must be perfect virginity and nothing less, and so on through all stages of growth.

IV. Thought-Absorption

I. Go away by yourself to some place where you will not be disturbed. Of course, not always and very rarely can you obtain this condition. Never mind. Do your best where you are and the great law will at least find for you all necessary conditions. Shut out all distracting conditions and impressions from the outer world. After a little effort you will be able to do so anywhere, at any time, and under any condition. All mental disturbance is within you.

II. Now relax, go passive, and draw off all tension from your nerves. Just you relax your mind and your body will follow suit. A few deep slow breaths will help the beginner.

III. Concentrate upon your mind inward steadily, calmly and with undivided attention.

IV. Fix your thought firmly upon your passive mind

and mentally say, 'You, my mind, are quite pure.' Think of this word (with all the ideas associated therewith) as sinking deeply into your mind and making a deep impress upon it as a die upon a wax. Let the outward form of the words 'pure,' 'fearless,' etc., sink into your mind.

V. Form a mental picture of yourself as if you already possessed all 'purity' and 'courage' and act them out in imagination. Make of it a pleasant 'day dream.'

VI. Intensify your relaxed condition of mind. Grow as 'limp' as a rag. Then mentally open yourself out to the inrush of all the Thought-Forces existing in the ether and connected with positive thoughts. The effort of this imagination to see this tremendous force pouring into your brain and body will actually put you en rapport with same.

VII. Now change from negative to a positive condition and say vigourously I am 'pure' and 'strong' Say it distinctly several times. Actually speak them out.

VIII. Then go out and live your thoughts out. This last is the most important condition.

IX. Practise this daily at the same hour and if possible at the same place, morning and evening. In fact hold the thought in your mind as often as possible till it becomes second Nature.

X. Use your power for good or you shall weep eternally. To misuse occult powers for mean, selfish, or low ends and to prostitute it into enslaving others weaker than yourselves mentally and physically is the greatest 'sin' man can commit against man.

II. Guru Worship

You get bigger by taking in and integrating things. In order to move forward faster, you need both abstract and specific goals. Man-worship is the key to all sudden and amazing spiritual growth. By "worshipping men," I mean loving, respecting, and being completely consumed by the idea of a Mahapurusha as the ideal man of realisation. All of these men were like Christ, Buddha, and Vivekananda. You should always and carefully think about the lives and works of heroes and saints. It's impossible to measure how much study and meditation shape and improve high ideas and goals. Man grows when his awareness expands and he learns new things. Any kind of study, whether it's subjective or objective, is a Tapashya, or austerity, that is meant to help you become wise. It's a way to honour Saraswati, the Goddess of Wisdom. One way to describe this worship is as complete emotional solitude, deep study, chastity and celibacy, and finally the merger of the personal and the impersonal. Living a simple life is the key to being great. You know how Archimedes raised his head and said, "Please do not disturb my circles," when he was threatened with death by the vandals who had come into his country? This man was doing Yoga without realising it. You have to be able to lose all awareness of this relative identity, which will die and change. Walt Whitman said that your personal ego "is contained within your hat and boots." Only then will you understand that you are unique in an infinite way. Man really finds himself when he loses himself. "You must be born again." The most important thing about studying this is not just how it shapes and forms people. Two objective ways to give strong ideas to the subjective self, or inner soul, are to study and directly hear the sound of a perfected soul. There is all information in the depths of the eternal subjective. The gate is locked, though. The master key that your Guru gives you lets you open the door and enter the gate of power and wisdom. You will be able to beat all pain and death once you get there. After that, you can help yourself. Man can only worship a God who is in some way bigger than him, not bigger in size. This kind of God he can "grow into." In Hinduism, the abstract ideas come from the God who is not a person, and the specific ideal comes from the Guru, who is God in human form. The first is needed for a mind that soars, and the second is needed to awaken and fuel a huge and unstoppable drive. Find both of them, and when you do, worship and serve them with all your heart. "I love my master like a dog loves its owner." I don't try to figure out what kind of person he is. It always surprises with how new and deep it is. This is what Vivekananda said about Ram Krishna. Do I need to tell you about the huge, all-powerful power that Vivekananda gained by worshipping the Guru? In India, the Guru only wants people to worship him, obey him, and do what he says, even though the master values and loves individual freedom more than anyone else. Pay attention to your master while you're at his feet like a sheep. In the same way, you will let his great inner power fill you up. Help him. Please be nice to him. Follow him. Serve him. No matter how many ways there are to be wrong. He has a great and deep nature that is full of contradictory traits. His personality is a riddle that you can't figure out by using logic and reason. If you want to understand him, you have to trust him completely and love and serve him like a loyal dog. You will also connect with his inner forces. You will be amazed at how brave and strong you are when he sends you out into the world to live out the great ideal he has set before you. You will own this world without fear, and every minute you will understand that only someone who has learned to obey can command. When I say "command," I don't mean "ruling over" someone or making them agree with you. This is the sign of a fool. As a result, your impact will naturally and irresistibly spread, drawing souls to the higher life. You will then stand as a tower of strength, a saviour of the race, an inspiration, and a living blessing to all people. Have peace! May you find strength in your soul!

Chapter 6
Presence, Discipline and Temperance

Personal magnetism is how each person expresses a subtle, compelling, and changing Force that makes them able to have an unusual effect on other people. These kinds of guys have been around all of you. They have amazing, almost supernatural abilities to convert, persuade, attract, fascinate, rule, and bend to their Will-Force men with very different personalities and mental traits. Men go out of their way to make women happy. Without even trying, they make people feel pulled to them, even when they don't want to. History gives us many examples of this kind of power.

What gives this power? How can you bring it out in yourself? Is it possible for everybody to get it? Has it been or could it be used for any better reason than to control other people's thoughts and make them do what you want on the relative level of existence? What is that higher use, then? One man I know is a Christian. His name is Mr. Krishna by name, who was in love with the young woman who worked as a magistrate's maid in Benares. This grown man went looking for a young college student who was naturally good at leading others and who was loved, admired, and respected by all of the other students, teachers, and professors. In his application, Mr. K. said, “I wish you would teach me mesmerism so that I can impress that girl.” In the end, Mr. K. got a harsh reprimand from the young mesmerist, who was really a born Yogi and didn’t care about the small things that people did or thought in this world. I think that almost all modern Western writers and teachers of this subject are only interested in the idea of making money through occultism. This is so true that the very word “occultism” makes a thoughtful man feel disgusted, repulsed, and horrified when he reads their work. Vivekananda said, “It is sin to show power.” A person who studies yoga and occultism only to develop, show, and showcase psychic and supernormal powers and siddhies will always end up in lust and be caught in a psychic machine of law and destructive thought forces that break him down. His spiritual growth is slowed down a lot, and he has to tread water again, which is very painful. It’s too easy for us to “impress” others, “strike terror” into others, and “psychologize” others in order to get what we want. If this sounds like you, please open your eyes to how stupid and bad you are. If you don’t, you shouldn’t be surprised if one day you meet a powerful thug who would not think twice about crushing you in any way possible. “Harm watch, harm catch.” I’m going to show you in real life what motivates a “Magnetic” personality and, when developed, turns any weak human into a god-like man.

Without a doubt, this power is not something that only a few divinely blessed people have. It can be grown by anyone. It’s inside you, but it needs to be stirred up very strongly before it can rise. Some men are born great, others become great because of unplanned events, and a third group becomes great by working hard and thinking things through.

Now, what are the causes behind Personal Influence?

I. Some say that the right control of the Sex-Force or Celibacy is the cause.

II. Others say that vegetarianism leads to it.

III. Still others assert that it is physical energy and nerve force.

IV. A fourth class has it that there emanates a current of magnetism from the human body and influences everyone coming within its "Magnetic field".

To start with the last point of view, I agree with some other top mental scientists that "magnetism," which has direct connections to the loadstone, is not the same thing as "human dynamic force."

Again, my own observations and those of others show beyond a doubt that "magnetic" personalities have incredibly well-trained and disciplined bodies, but this force is almost never coming from a huge, bulky body with big, ugly muscles. There is no doubt that it is not just physical power and energy. A slim, active, and strong body is desired, and anyone can get it. If you want to eat something healthy, like fruits, nuts, maize and veggies, you should eat them. They have rhythmic properties that help you build a fine, sensitive body that can handle more mental and physical stress than animal 'carcass' ever could. In the early stages of organic evolution, matter does have an effect on thought. However, this effect is mostly reversed once CONSCIOUS evolution starts. Therefore, vegetarianism is not a strict and necessary requirement in this case, even though it is highly recommended from a scientific point of view for the growth of a healthy, active, and polished body. As one mental scientist puts it, some of the most "magnetic" people make "graveyards out of their stomachs."

Last but not least, Bramhacharya, or celibacy, which is practiced by Sannyasis in India, is purely spiritual, but it has a lot to do with Personal Magnetism. I'd tell the average man, "Strive for CONTINENCE, chastity, and control in this direction." It would be a waste of force to emasculate someone. It's better if this force is strong. All Sannyasis learn, whether they are aware of it or not, how to change this energy into mental and spiritual force. Usually, their thoughts live on a level of mental and spiritual effort where there is no sensuality or grossness at all. They have completely gone beyond these things. This is true for all educated thinkers, philosophers, and workers, married or single. When I hear the word "philosophy," it makes me think of purity, holiness, and godliness.

But while all four of those claims are partly true, they

are not at all what they seem to be. This is what the question comes down to: "What makes one man better than another?" Nature studies show that the higher level of mind manages the lower level. People who led the way, like Napoleon, Alexander, and others, were always ahead of their time. But they worked hard for small things, and we don't think they succeeded. Let's go out further. In the past, Buddha, Christ, Zoroaster, and many others had great influence on men. In current times, Vivekananda and a few others have done the same. By reading about their lives and works, you try to figure out what made them so heroic in the first place.

If I were asked to sum up the secrets of their Power I would say:

(1) "Their Intelligence and Thought-Power. (2) Awakened Will-Power and Self-Control."

I. It was by their intelligence that they could take fearless possession of the world, handle men and women easily, read human nature at a glance and "be all things to all men," i.e.., put their fingers direct on the spiritual, mental, and physical necessities of widely varying temperaments and help each right where he stood in the ladder of evolution.

II. It was by their developed thought-force that they drew the whole world to themselves. The positive thinker generates a force that draws all such as are negative to him. Nearly the whole world was negative to these Masters and hence felt attracted to them. These were the human touchstones.

III. It was by their strong, manly, marvellous Will-Power that they drove their suggestions into other minds and gained an immediate ascendency over whatever environments they were placed in. The whole man is summed up in his Will. Every other power in man is subservient to the Will. And say what you will, it is this power more than any other that we respect in others. It is the central staff in our character. Intelligence is the directive energy. Will-Power is the propulsive energy. And the latter when wielded under the guidance of the former makes of man a veritable God.

IV. It was by their unusual power of Self-control that they could stand square upon their feet and could remain unshaken by the waves of conflicting opinions and the hostile attacks that continually dashed up against them. Master yourself, i.e., your personal, relative and lower self, and beyond the shadow of a doubt, the mastery of others is already yours. But the world will teach you bitter lessons and rend you to pieces if you try consciously to control it while you are still a slave to your lower self. Be great. Strive for Perfection. So will you be recognised by others. And according to the transcendent energy of the highest law of our Being it is the consciousness of heights scaled, accomplishments achieved and consequent dawning of a Loftier Ideal upon our intellectual horizon that fills us with Strength and Peace rather than the recognition of our worth by others. It is a serious mistake to care for fame, praise and admiration. You get them only when you do not care for them in the least, when your soul has outgrown all such clinging to the relative in the light of eternal thought, when you have risen to the Absolute and learnt to read the meaning of the "LARGER WORLD" of life. Do not pass by this lightly. In it is the key to Peace, Power and Poise. All that is Real and Permanent, is on the plane of the Absolute.

Now we are drawing to the practical side of our Lesson. The four principal points, you will please remember, are: (1) Intelligence. (2) Thought-Force. (3) Will-Power. (4) Self-Control. You might feel surprised at my retailing this "ancient history" instead of teaching you how to approach a man, make him your slave and command him to fall down at your feet and do your bidding. Perhaps you expected me to tell you how to sail through the air, pass through solid walls, materialize and dematerialize at will and like Appolonius of Tyana vanish in the flash of an eye from the court of Ionysius and appear elsewhere at a distance of 19,000 miles at the same moment. No, no. I will take it for granted that you are made of different stuff and an earnest seeker after the truth. If you strive to build yourself on the basis of the simple principles as laid down in this series of lessons you will in time grow into the Higher Self and at last become one with it. Moreover, your daily life will be the Occasion for the practical application of these principles, thus enabling you to pursue your way through life calmly, earnestly, independently and with the quiet dignity of a man "who knows what he is about". I cannot and would not speak of "get-rich-quick" methods of self-development because they are the veriest rot imaginable.

Now then: (1) Intelligence and (2) Thought-Force are the natural results of an organised brain.

Concentration is the key to such development. Concentration has been fully explained in Lesson No. 1. By the constant exercise of concentration, objectively and subjectively, in your daily life you will in a short time become conscious of growing Strength. The exercises I give you in this lesson on Self-Control, Will-Culture and Memory-Culture if gone through with perseverance will further develop Concentrative ability. In fact, this entire series of lessons will call for Effort and Concentration. "Rome was not built in a day"-- nor can you achieve real greatness in a few months. No. All I can do is to indicate the line and the nature of the effort required of you and if clearly followed, Progress and Growth will commence from the first day. In connection with this, a little digression would be necessary. The Occultist says: Nature, unaided, fails. The purposiveness of Deity, manifesting in nature an evolution, is present in all individual centres but it has the way to full expression opened out to itself only when the more evolved centres of life consciously cooperate with it. Evolution is started and carried only by the creation of centres within the GREAT CONSCIOUSNESS and by preserving and enlarging or expanding these centres.

So long as the race had not reached "SELF-CONSCIOUSNESS" (see Yoga Lessons) the sub-conscious forces of nature had entire control over evolutionary processes, but this stage was reached by the race according to the LAW Of AVERAGES in the seventeenth century and you are now expected to take your progress in your hands and consciously direct your inner forces along such lines as best correspond to the stage of your growth. So independent study and steady thinking form the secrets of a keen and broad intelligence. You will always find that the man who is more powerful than yourself and moves you at his will has an intelligence and understanding far superior to yours and he can read your whole nature as he would an open book, although you find him quite beyond your depth. Learn to regard earnestly the workings of different mentalities around you. Become a student of human nature. To you, each man ought to be only a partial expression of his mind. Examine closely into the motives acting behind each personality. Learn to respond more quickly to the Thoughts and Feelings of a man than to his outer speech and action. The latter are objective expressions of the subjective self. The study of Phrenology and Physiognomy are good things to start with in your efforts to acquire knowledge of human nature. Mind is One and at the same time,

Many. Subjectively, it is ONE. Objectively; many. So by looking impartially into "yourself" in the calm light of the intellect and through silent introspection, you will always find a clue to the working bases of other minds. Each man is a puzzle and most of all are YOU a puzzle unto yourself. Solve either and you have solved both. "MAN, KNOW THYSELF."

The Secret of the Will

The power to act is called will-force. All of the other mental processes can be turned on or off by it. In terms of what it does, the JUDGEMENT has the most impact on this ability. Will-Power shows up as Desire on the lower level of thought, and it is affected by both outside attractions and repulsions. The Will is not free on this plane. But when it draws the will to show itself to the outside world from within, based on higher reason, then it really is will-power. The human will is a slave on the material plane, but a king or queen on the spiritual plane. Then we could call it the "awakened" will. I believe that the eternal sword-switching between the Determinists and the Libertarians can only be stopped by having a good understanding of how people are spiritually. Until then, I believe that both groups' cases are strong. Every side has a piece of the truth, but we need the balancing light of spiritual psychology to see the whole truth for what it is. For now, though, I want to stress that your will is only truly free when it is self-determined, that is, when it has risen above the urges of the Lower Personal Self and acts in line with the

Higher Impersonal Self. This is the most important fact that you need to remember. Let us quickly talk about the "I aM" consciousness. Don't just ignore this as a bunch of dry rot. If someone doesn't understand the "I AM" consciousness, they will never be able to create real spiritual Will-Force. So please pay close attention and think about what follow.

"I"

You will become aware of the "I" if you just go inside and look at the report your awareness gives you about the self-dwelling within. But if you look a little more closely, you will see that this "I" can be broken down into two separate parts that can work together but can also be thought of separately. There is a "I" function and a "me" function, and different things happen in these mental twins. The first is the "masculine" principle, and the second is the "feminine" principle. These words are also used in new works about psychology: Conscious Mind, Active Mind, Voluntary Mind, Objective Mind, and so on. All of these have to do with the "I" concept. The "me" form of mind is the same as the Passive Mind, the Subjective Mind, the Sub-Conscious Mind, and so on. There are 99 people in the world who mean this "me" when they say "I." Let us now look at what this "me" means. It is mostly made up of our minds, bodies, and the physical senses that come from touch, smell, taste, sight, and sound. For some of us, the physical and sexual parts of life are very connected to our minds. People and I "live there." Some guys also think of their "clothes" as an important part of who they are. Humans start to "dissociate" their idea of "me" from their bodies as consciousness grows, though. They start to see their bodies as friends and as "belonging to" them. His thoughts, feelings, likes and dislikes, habits, traits, and characteristics then help him figure out who he is. But over time, he starts to understand that even these feelings can change, that they can be born and die, and that they are affected by the Principles of Rhythm and Polarity. He has a vague idea that he can change them by willpower and "transmute" them into completely different mental states. Then he starts to "dissociate" himself from his emotions and feelings again, and finally, by thinking about them, focusing, and analysing them, he separates them into the "not I" group. He starts to understand that he is more than his body and feelings at that point. The same is true for the intellectual processes. Intellectual men often believe that their minds are separate from their bodies and emotions, but that they are still in charge of those parts of themselves. "Self-Consciousness" is the name of this stage. "I am in charge of my feelings and body." But as intellectual man's awareness grows, he discovers that he can stand back and watch (mentally, of course) his mind go through different intellectual processes. If you study psychology and logic, you'll understand how all of your thoughts can be held at arm's length, looked at, analysed, named, and talked about with the same ease that the professor talks about solid, liquid, and acrid substances in his lab. He finally realises that even the Intellect's great skills have to be put in the "not I" collection. This is almost as far as the average man can see. You may realise that "I am not the body, not the emotions, not the intellect." So, you can see that the "me," or Feminine or Passive mental principle, is the part of your awareness that is made up of all of your physical, emotional, and intellectual functions. The "I" or Masculine Function is what can think of itself as different from all of these things. But we need to take another step. What you were taught to think of as the Spiritual Consciousness (see "Spiritual Consciousness") will also end up in the "Not-I" or "me" group. To sum up, the spiritual mind is made up of everything GOOD, NOBLE, and GREAT in the mental field. At the moment, it is the "Super-Conscious" mind. But take note: the "I" will lose its sense of relativity and separation when it has evolved further and mastered this field of consciousness as well, being able to see it as the last of the "me" collections. At that point, it will have reached the "I AM" consciousness, which is the true individuality. How do I say this? This "I AM" is not the ego's spoiled act of self-assertion. "I" but really means GOD CONSCIOUSNESS as perfect Being, perfect Knowing, or perfect Happiness. It means coming to know an infinite and eternal self or individuality. "He who has lost himself has gained himself." This is how it works: When the "I" consciousness is linked to the PERSONALITY that comes from the "me" consciousness, it is stuck on the relative plane. They can only think with one brain and feel happiness with one body. The happiness they feel is temporary, short-lived, and unreliable because this world of relative life is always changing. Only the fact that it changes makes it lasting. This means that thought and wanting are both limited and not free as long as the "I" thinks and wants only for its own good.

But once it has connected with the Spiritual mind and wants to work for the Larger Self, the "I AM," it has to give up the personal self and follow the direction of the impersonal Higher Self. Walt Whitman said, "I refuse to be sealed up in my hat and boots." "I am the absolute" (Aham Brahmasmi) is not what the Vedantist means when he says it. No, no. He's not made that way. Self-consciousness is no longer a part of his life. He has lost touch with his specific "I" and has become one with the absolute "I AM," the generic, intangible, eternal, all-powerful Self that is everything and everyone. This "I am" is the Spirit or Atman. There can only be one Individuality, and that is the Absolute. It is objectively shown in people as Cosmic Consciousness. In my opinion, it is God. You now have a sense of what "I am" Consciousness is. Do not give up. This is your true, bigger self. To understand and use Will-Power, the "I" or the Positive Mental Principle is the most important thing. You need to know the other one in order to use the first one. The power of will is in your soul. As I said above, this "I" is opposite to the "I AM" or God, which both mean the same thing. When it comes to the Higher Self, it's good. This "I" is what the "I AM" says will happen in the future. Even though it will lose itself while it finds itself, every child does the same thing when it grows up. On a spiritual level, Christ was one with his Father-in-Heaven, which is why he could calm the waves and bring the dead back to life. But just look at what Lord Christ's Will-Force is like. Think about how he would always go into the Silence to get ideas for his work in the objective world. Again, notice how he has complete disregard for and power over himself. Did he care if his body lived or died? Did he live for getting pleasure from his body? Did he "play to the gallery" and do and say things to get something in return? No! He had forgotten about his own needs because he was so excited about the cause of the Eternal Spirit. He wasn't moved by a weak sense of what was right and wrong. He found the "Motives" that gave him strength in the life of action from within. Nothing from the outside, from the world of less appealing things, could even slightly change his mind or make him lose focus. Are you or can you get ready to follow his lead? So, my first point, and the only surefire way to get your Will-Power going is this:

A. Teach Thy Will to "Resist and Renounce." Strengthen your Will-Power by Renunciation. By Resistance is not meant outer resistance or aggressiveness. I find that all the modern teachers of Hypnotism advise their students to develop Will-Power by exercising it upon others. This is placing the cart before the horse. We Hindus know better. No; by Resistance to and Repression of your lower Desire-Nature is meant letting the more difficult choice exercise its compelling and restraining power over the easier one. Says Sister Nivedita: "The Indian ideal is that man whose lower mind is so perfectly under control that he can at any moment plunge into the thought-ocean and remain there at will without the least possibility of a sudden break and unexpected return to the life of the senses." Yes, your interests should be within and not without. You must rise above all personal impulse. Even in this world you find that men of distinction, fame and honour have achieved recognition by practising a little self-denial, which is a "milder" form of absolute Renunciation as practised by true Sanyasis. The man who can work at his aim with perseverance and denies himself the mess of pottage of present indulgence in view of some future gain develops Will-Power. So in training your Will to 'resist', you must, as a first step, sternly refuse to indulge impulses, desires and tendencies not in consonance with the dictates of your Higher Self. You must actually go out of your way and "deny" yourself the little or great "comforts" to which you are or have been accustomed. The strongest-willed man is he who has the greatest control over his inclinations, and who can 'force' himself to do such things as he is naturally most inclined to do. This is a characteristic which cannot be developed in a day. There are some children and even grown-up men and women who mistake their 'obstinacy' for Will-Power. They want a thing and when they do not get it they tear their hair, gnash their teeth, stamp their feet and fly into a terrible passion. Since people think that these uncontrolled creatures are strong-willed while all that you could say about them is that they are utter slaves to their desires. You must practise self-denial in fifty different ways and force yourself to do certain things, 'little and big,' every day purely for developing this power of Resistance. No short-cut to this. Some children develop it unconsciously by 'forcing' themselves to study when they might play, and by applying themselves to such studies as are dry and uninteresting to them they thus practise voluntary Concentration. Practise self-denial in every possible way. Cut off such luxuries as you think "you must have." "Take a cold bath when you would prefer a warm one. Arise promptly in the morning. Make yourself call upon people you have avoided. Stand up in a street car when you would prefer sitting; walk when it is convenient to ride. Make engagements with yourself and keep them. Promise yourself that when you see something to be done you will spring at once to it however strong may be the inclination to put it off awhile" and back of it all let there be the auto-suggestion: "I am doing all these hard things in order to build up my Will-Power and each time 'I' succeed in forcing 'my mind' to do a thing or not to do it I make the next victory easier and my Will-Power stronger." Of course the above is only a hint as to your line of practise.

B. You must not give yourself such hard tasks of Self-Development as might be too heavy and beyond the present strength of your Will. In denying yourself you develop self-control. In forcing yourself to do certain things you develop powers of Self-Expression. In one the Will moves along negative lines. In the other along positive lines. Both are necessary. The man who cannot control and command himself can never develop and express Himself. But be sure to begin with easy things and then as you gain in confidence you may attempt more difficult feats.

C. The faculties of Courage and Confidence are essentially important. Nothing weakens the will so much as Fear and lack of Self-Confidence. Self-Confidence is not blustering self-conceit. That within you which says "I CAN" when calmly and doggedly backed by your "I Will" when deliberately translated into action develops Will-Force and commands startling results.

D. Always hold these words before your passive Mind:

1. Earnestness. 2. Determination. 3. Courage.
4. Confidence. 5. Stick-to-itiveness. 6. Patience.
7. I can and I will.

E. The tendency of the Masculine function of your mind to "I" is towards giving, expressing or projecting energy; that of the Feminine is towards generating and creating mental progeny such as thoughts, mental energy, new habits, etc. It is why the Feminine Principle has been called the "mental womb" by ancient philosophers. It comprises also the faculty of Imagination. The Masculine function does the work of the 'Will' in its varied phases. The Feminine function receives impressions and generates mental offspring in the form of new thoughts, ideas, concepts, thought-habits and so forth. Its powers of creative energy are strikingly marvellous and have been proved and attested to in Psychological experiments conducted by the best known mental scientists of the day. But "positive" mental energy must be projected by the 'I' into the Passive Mind through concentration, suggestion and willing before the latter can be started to work along any line of creative effort. This suggestion may be given by you to your sub-conscious mind or it may come as an outer impression. Unless you control your Passive Mind, it is sure to be controlled by others. Then you are a slave. Now in cultivating the above seven qualities, you should take up one word at a time and let the outer form sink into your mind. Place yourself in a relaxed and passive condition. Close your eyes and picture the form of the word to yourself, for instance, D-E-T-E-R-M-I-N-A-T-I-O-N. Employ the Imagination and visualize mentally. This done, i.e., when the word-picture is well photographed upon your mind and fastened in place, your next step will be to picture yourself the Ideas, qualities, physical and mental characteristics, etc., associated with the word. Your third step is to calmly, concentratedly and confidently command your Passive Mind to generate that quality. Remember, your mind will at first rebel, but a very little persistence will lead to complete success. Repeat the auto-suggestions daily at the same time. See that it manifests in Action. Act it out as often as possible. Of course your efforts will be imperfect to begin with, but, never mind, go ahead, keeping firm hold on your "I can and I will" in spite of all things and success is quite certain. Once you have developed these seven qualities, you can do anything.

F. Do not let your friends or anyone--no matter who!-deflect you from your resolutions. “Let not thy right hand know what thy left hand does.” Talk never. Let results show. The Lord has hidden himself best and His work is wonderful beyond compare! Your very friends and relatives will spit upon you for lacking any of these qualities. Do not ever impose your will upon others, but never let others to impose upon you against the sanction of your own judgment. In fact, none can unless you are a weakling and fickle-minded.

G. Frequent the company of chaste, strong-willed men and you cannot but grow strong.

H. Read Literature on this subject and obtain all possible aid through Knowledge.

I. If your faculty of imagination and idealism are undeveloped, cultivate them, because it is these two that make a god of a man. Philosophers, scholars, poets and musicians have them well-developed. But where imagination is uncontrolled by higher reason and where idealism is not backed by a strong will, there you have the idle ‘dreamer of dreams’ and such a state of mind is reprehensible and pitiable indeed!

J. Will-Power grows by faith in one’s ability by exercise; by devotion to the UNCONDITIONED SPIRIT.

K. In your efforts to develop Will-Power, be not afraid that your health will break down. In fact, Perfect Health is the result of a perfect Will. Deny the power of disease and weakness over yourself. "I can never be ill. My body is my slave. It shall always manifest perfect health." Convince your passive mind--which has charge of your body--of this by repeated commands, demands and assertions. Always think of your body as being as strong as adamant. Never talk of either health or disease or weakness. You must be above caring for these. They are your Natural rights. Only when you lower yourself they have power to trouble you. Go beyond the lower self. Your business is to care for the Higher-Self--that in which "You" live, move, and have your being. Also teach and train your Will to move along negative lines of self-repression as well as along positive lines of Self-Expression. Balance both. The former precedes the latter. Now I will pass on to the subject of SELF-CONTROL, with the distinct understanding that Self-Control and Will-Power are inextricably bound up in each other. You Get the real "practical work" in the endeavour for Self-Control.

Self-Control

Rightly has it been remarked that is easy to talk of and write upon this subject but most difficult to possess it. Perfect Self-Control means infinite power. Only the Buddas and the Christs of this World manifested

Perfect Self-Control. "Anything short of the absolute control of thought, word and deed is only sowing wild oats," said Vivekananda. It is with no little diffidence that I approach this subject as whoever handles this subject is rightly culpable as being a "Do-as-I-say-and-not-as-I-do" class of writers. Still you can make appreciable progress in this direction by mastering these instructions, going through the exercises and last but most important by "carrying the principles in your mind" and applying them as far as you can in your daily life. Nothing is more conducive to rapid growth and development as the making of the "little and big" affairs in your work-a-day life, the occasion for the practical expression and conscious translation of your ideals. We all are guilty of a serious mistake in setting apart our higher ideals for regular 'practice' hours and leading a life of low and quite different ideals in our ordinary life. The natural process, as you can see, is to LIVE OUT your highest ideals every minute of your life. Nothing is more important than the daily occupation of a man and if he fails to bring his ideals right into these little things, then Success will ever elude him. A mental scientist has summed up the entire secret of Character-Building in this valuable advice on Objective Concentration: the simple task of mental concentration on whatever task, business or profession a man is engaged in is the beginning of the mastery which is the perfection of Objective Concentration. Whatever you are doing be master of your work. If you are a cobbler mend shoes in a perfect manner; if a barber keep your razors and scissors in a state that will excite the admiration of your customers; if a tailor make the coat fit like a glove; if a clerk keep your accounts in apple-pie order; if a builder scorn your jerry-brother; if a singer enchant the listener with a concord of sweet sounds; if an actor enter into the spirit of the character and make the play-goer feel that

"All the world's a stage
And all the men and women merely players,
They have their exits and their entrance
And one man in his time plays many parts."

If you're a leader in any area of thought or action, remember that what you give is equal to what you receive. You are responsible for the lives and happiness of your followers, whether you know it or not, and thousands of people may secretly curse your incompetence and messiness. Being a good cobbler is much better than being a bad boss.

If you carefully follow the advice above, I think you will be ready to enter the higher levels of mastery. Do not forget to take it to heart. Believe it or not, a person who constantly gives up when things don't go as planned, expects quick results, and thinks there is a royal way to learn Mental Science will never get very far. In fact, his eagerness will make him fail. No one's life is complete without doing something useful. The Yogi who has given up the world is ahead of the curve and has already done his job. The real monk and the real saint are the world's Pillars of Strength. I can't say this enough times. The fact that they breathe the same air as you is a blessing and an immeasurable benefit to the race.

Preliminary Steps

According to Mr. Atkinson, the first thing that is needed for centering is the ability to block out outside ideas, sights, and sounds; to stop being distracted; and to have complete control over your body and mind. The mind needs to be able to direct the body, and the body needs to be able to direct the mind. The will itself is strong enough, but the mind needs to be made stronger by putting it directly under the spell of the will. Mind gets stronger when the will pushes it, so it can send out thought vibrations much more effectively, and those vibrations have a lot more of an impact.

The first four tasks are meant to train the mind to understand and follow its own instructions. Take them in your room alone and don't tell anyone else about them. Don't forget about them either, even if they seem simple. If you are one of those stupid guys who talk about their workouts in order to get compliments, you will never be successful. Take your work seriously and do it with all your heart. For good, give up being changeable, and learn to build Power in quiet and through work. You get the power to "work" through prayer. The answer comes from your "larger self," which is the Spirit of God "brooding" over everything and giving everyone strength. But don't disrespect DEITY by thinking it will "do the work" for you while you relax after praying. Not true. That person prays who works nonstop, quietly, calmly, smartly, and without stopping.

Exercise 1

Relax your whole body, then hold your neck, shoulders, and head in a straight line. Cross your legs under each other so that your weight rests comfortably on your ribs. Place your right hand on your right leg and your left hand on your left leg. In every part of the body, the muscles should not move at all. Keep in mind that you should avoid making your body stiff or tense. Muscles shouldn't have to work hard at all. There's no need to "relax" at all. First, give it 5 minutes. Keep going until you can sit for 5 minutes without thinking about it. Then, increase the time to 15 minutes, which is about all you need. The goal is to give you complete control over all muscle moves that you can't stop. Additionally, it is a great "rest-cure" after mental or physical activity that makes you tired. "STILLNESS" is the most important thing, and you can practise it anywhere, even while sitting in a chair. The goal is to "relax" and be physically and mentally calm. Don't let the fact that this exercise seems easy fool you. It's not so simple after all. You can easily lose track of your body and stay still for a long time by focusing your mind on a certain train of thoughts or ideas or connecting your mind to the larger self. Scientists and psychologists have found that forgetting about yourself can lead to creativity, inspiration, and intelligence. People told Vivekananda that when he sits down to meditate, "in 10 minutes he becomes quite unconscious of the body, even though it may be black with mosquitoes." Do you get it now? For deep focus to work, you have to completely forget about your body. It's what Dr. Fahnestock called the "STATUVOLIC" state, which means that the willpower is really strong and the "outer self" is completely put aside and forgotten.

Exercise 2

In your daily life, try to keep a calm and collected attitude. Avoid acting tense, strained, worried, or fidgety, and don't look like you're too stressed out. Take it easy, be sure of yourself, and walk with respect. Be polite, thoughtful, and quiet. Getting mental exercise and Will-Culture will help you learn how to behave properly. Stop moving your hands and feet around or rocking back and forth in your chair while you talk or sit. Do not chew your moustache, bite your nails, roll your tongue in your mouth, or do any other action that is not necessary while you are learning, reading, or writing. It may have become "second nature" for you to do these things. Do not jerk or twitch your body. Don't blink or look blank. You should practise being able to handle quick and loud noises without getting upset. These kinds of actions show a lack of control. Don't let anything outside (or even inside) of you make you lose your cool. In a talk, your voice should be even and your speech should be calm and measured. There should always be a certain amount of backup. To sum up, always keep yourself well under control. In order to get this balance, you should always think about "Firmness," "Self-Control," and "Self-Respect," and let these thoughts show in how you act. Don't bluster, brag, gossip, jokes, too much laughter, energy, and other such things. When you laugh too much, your will gets weak. Be an honest thinker who stays quiet. Pay attention. Think of "solitude" as the best way to grow as a person.

Exercise 3

Fill a wine glass with water, and then hold it between your fingers while extending your arm straight out in front of you. Keep your eyes on the glass and try to keep your arm so still that you can't see it move. Start with a one-minute workout and keep going until you hit five minutes. Switch between your right and left arms. Take it up to 15 minutes.

Exercise 4

While sitting in your chair, keep your back straight, chin out, and your head up. Lift your right arm up so that it is straight out in front of you and level with your shoulders. Look at your hand with your eyes closed and turn your head around. Hold your arm still for one minute. Do it again with your left arm. Slowly lengthen the time until it reaches 5 minutes. Hands should be held with the palms facing down.

The tasks that follow are meant to help you get your mind in check, which will allow you to move on your own.

Exercise 5

Place your hands on a table in front of you with your arms clenched and the back of your hand on the table, with your thumb crossed over your fingers. Look at the hand for a while, and then slowly extend the thumb. The whole time, keep your eyes on the action as if it were the most important thing in the world. Then slowly spread out your first finger, then your second, and so on, until all of your fingers are spread out and open. Then do the opposite, starting with the little finger and working your way up until the fist is back where it was, with the thumb closed over the fingers. Do it again with your left hand. Do this practice five times while sitting down, then increase the number of times to ten. Don't forget to keep your full attention on how the fingers are moving. That's the main thing.

Exercise 6

Place the middle fingers of one hand between the middle fingers of the other hand. Do not touch the thumbs. After that, slowly twist your hands around each other in a circle. Make sure you keep your eyes on the very end of your hands.

Note: Exercises 3, 4, 5, and 6 are from the writings of Yogi Ramacharaka, with some changes I made.

Exercise 7

Going alone into a dark room and focusing on one thing for forty-eight hours after the full moon every month is advised. Hold this thought for as long as you can without letting anything else come to mind. At first, it will be hard to focus because your mind will keep jumping from one thing to another. But if you keep at it, you'll be able to think about one thing for a long time. This should be done for five nights in a row, for an hour each night.

Exercise 8

Find a clear night sky and spend some time outside every night. Try to count as many stars as you can without thinking about anything else. When it comes to growth, the more stars you can count without thinking about it, the better. That was a pretty cool practice.

Exercise 9

Take 12 regular rocks. Put them in your left hand. Then, with your right hand, pick up one rock and hold it at arm's length. For sixty seconds, don't let any other thoughts cross your mind. The same goes for all the rocks. Then use your left hand to pick up. Do this every day for an hour.

Exercise 10

Keep your mind focused on someone far away and don't let any other ideas enter. May he become strong, healthy, and pious. Picture your subject in your mind as if they were sitting right in front of you. Then make strong, honest, and positive ideas to his subconscious mind. Wish that he would feel sorry for you, write you about it, and honestly work with you to become spiritually new. Be cool and sincere about it.

Exercise 11

Spread some wet sand out over an area about a yard square. Make it really smooth. Then, use your index finger to make any shapes or images you want in the sand. Like, a square, a triangle, or any other shape. Focus your attention on this person. After that, calmly focus your mind on that one thing and wish that the thought form that you make by focusing be sent to someone who can sense your will. Each day for 15 minutes, do this the same way until your subject gets it. As you ask him to sit still and calmly in the silence, keep your mind open. You should face the north, south, east, or west way where you want to send your thought. Imagine that you and your subject are linked by a mental wire, and keep your aim straight. Remember that the Will-Power is shown by a straight line because it goes straight to its goal.

Exercise 12

Every night before retiring, concentrate upon your passive mind: "When I get up in morning, my Will-power and Thought-Force will have increased. I expect you to bring about a thorough change in my Will-Force. It will gain in vigour, resolution, firmness and confidence. It must grow strong, strong, strong." Project these positive suggestions into your subjective self earnestly, confidently and concentrated ly. You will progress quickly by leaps and bounds. Every morning shall find you stronger and full of vim, sap and energy. Persevere, persevere. In following up such ideals to a successful conclusion you must have an (i) overpowering desire; (ii) a strong belief in your ability to accomplish anything; (iii) an invincible determination not a backboneless 'I will try to'; (iv) earnest expectation. This is an important and an infallible method in Will-development.

Exercise 13

Go into a room by yourself where no one will bother you. 'Relax' all over at the start. Then don't think about anything else while you count from one to ten. Your mind is open to new ideas as soon as you finish this. Just focus like you did before, and tell your subconscious mind to create a strong memory that can't be lost. Make your own ideas for things.

Exercise 14

Pick out six faces you don't know. Make them stick in your mind very strongly. Then think of them at least once a day for a year, making at least one more person smile every day. If you find that you forget some of your older names, don't add any new ones. Instead, focus on the ones you already know to make sure you don't forget them. This task is really interesting. Remember that memories are stored in the subconscious mind.

Exercise 15

Focus your attention on a passage in a holy book and try to remember it. Every day, learn one phrase by heart, and don't forget the old ones. Over time, you will get much better.

Exercise 16

People who have trouble remembering things always have trouble focusing. Attention is the key to having a strong mind. As you can see, the tasks above are pretty dull and boring. But the only way to train your "attention" is to do boring and light activities. People with a strong will can handle even the most boring and repetitive jobs without getting tired. You need to give yourself things that might look like "work" to you. Always keep in mind that the work you put into focusing on boring, dry, and repetitive tasks on purpose builds Willpower and "mental muscle." This will give you strong power over your body and mind, and you will be "Master" over your lower urges. When you have power over yourself, you will also have power over other people. If you can keep yourself in check, it will be easy to get other people to do what you want. But remember that this holy power should only be used to help others grow, improve, and become stronger. Try your Will on your personality in every way possible, and be happy with anything less than full power. Your goal should be to have complete control over "self." I've told you the real tricks. To use your creativity and knowledge to help yourself grow, you have to use them yourself. You need to finish the fight on your own. Get up and start working on your project today, not tomorrow. In the back of your mind, always keep this good incentive and auto-suggestion in mind:

"This is to Develop my Will-Power and No Temporary Pain can Equal the Power and Happiness Arising Out of Self-Control."

Get a strong grip on your feelings. Don't let this natural force use you, but do use it. If you can control your speech, you can control your emotions. Always get right to the point. Practice being quiet. Hold back volubility. When you talk and write, be short. Don't get upset. Maintain a level head and focus.

Gleanings from Professor James on the Law of Habit

From a physiological point of view, a learned habit is just a new way for certain incoming currents to leave the brain.

The great thing is to turn our nerve system into a friend instead of an enemy.--Just like we should avoid the plague, we should also avoid ways that are likely to hurt us.

It's better for our higher mental abilities to be free to do their own work when we can let automata handle more of the little things in our daily lives. There is no person who is more unhappy than someone who is always unsure of what to do and who has to expressly think about every action, like getting up and going to bed or starting a new piece of work.

Maxim I: When we start a new thought or let go of an old one, we should make sure to do so with as much strength and determination as possible.

Maxim II: Don't let an exception happen until the new habit is deeply ingrained in your life.

Each slip-up is like letting a ball of string fall while carefully wrapping it up; one slip-up means more than a lot of turns will have to be made again.

The best way to make sure that the nervous system always does the right thing is to keep teaching it. The most important thing is to never lose a fight. Every gain on the bad side cancels out the good gains on the right.

The most important safety measure is to control the other powers so that one can have a string of uninterrupted successes until repetition has made it strong enough to handle the resistance no matter what.

It is very important to make sure of success right away. Being great all the time is what it takes.

Be careful not to give the will a task that will guarantee its failure right away. If you can handle it, a short period of pain followed by some free time is what you should aim for, whether you're giving up opium or just changing the times you wake up or work.

It's crazy how quickly a wish will go away on its own if it's not fed.

There is no such thing as buildup of ethical forces without steady progress. Regular work makes this possible and trains and habits us for it. Maxim III: Act on every decision you make and every emotional push you may feel in the direction of the habits you want to form as soon as possible.

In the moment that they produce motor effects, not when they are being formed, is when resolves and aims tell the brain about the new "set."

One thing that is needed for the lever to work is for the real chance to actually be there. This is how the moral will can gain strength and rise above itself. If someone has nothing solid to push against, they will never get past the point of making empty gestures.

If you let a resolve or a fine glow of feeling go away without doing anything useful, it's a waste and a chance lost. It works to stop future resolves and emotions from going their natural course of discharge.

When we let our feelings go, they can get in the way of going away.

Worship of the Terrible

The soul shouldn't let the lower nature or the "Personal Self" confuse it. Instead, it should seek Death and not life, throwing itself on the point of the sword and becoming one with the terrible. Those who are chosen by the Lord to carry the fire of spirit will have all their sense pleasures turn to ashes and their eyes will be crushed by the hollowness of Maya's mortal life.

When a lion is hit in the heart, it lets out its loudest roar. When a snake is hit in the head, it raises its hood.

And the beauty of the soul only shows itself when a person is deeply hurt.

To do is the Western ideal, while to suffer is the Eastern ideal. The ideal life would have a balance of doing good things without any attachment and going through bad things. Honour the terrible. You should honour death, sorrow, and pain just because they are there. But this isn't the cry of a coward, a suicide, or a weakling who loves Death morbidly. It's the cry of a philosopher who has heard everything and knows very well how pointless it is to want happiness on the relative plane of limits. Don't forget St. Francis of Assisi's victory cry: "WELCOME, SISTER DEATH!" "Be a witness" means to the things that happen but not to them. Keep the power to stay detached at all times for yourself. Do not accept anything, no matter how nice it is, if it hides a chain in your soul. At the drop of a hat, be ready to cut any link that suggests a soul relationship. Don't think about anything. Do not change your will. You man, reach the impersonal standpoint! That's the only place where you can find true happiness on a personal level. Who or what dies and comes back to life?--Your personality, your lower self.

"Sometimes naked, sometimes mad,
Now as a scholar, again as a fool
Here a rebel, there a saint,
Thus they appear on the earth
-the Perfect Ones. Paramhamsas"--Viveka Chudamani.

If you believe what your feelings tell you, you will say "soul for nature." But if you can see things from a spiritual point of view, you will say "no-nature for soul." Nature has evolution, decline, and involution, and they will all happen over and over again forever. All of this is happening only because the soul wants to show itself. But that kind of speech can only come from a soul that lives on its own plane. Say, "Money, not I, is my slave." Say, "Nature, not I, is my slave." Give up your body, your life, and all your wants for fun on the relative plane. In the same way, you will go beyond all limits. You are really infinite and absolute. When you limit your nature to the "particular self," that's when you become bound and sad. It's like being a slave to life and death, happiness and pain, and so on, on the relative plane. This is the end. "Survival of the Fittest" is the rule here, and competition is your slave. Please don't let the bright lights of modern society blind you. You are eating things that were made from your brother's blood. You are "Slave--Slave--Slave" to a breath of air, food, life, death, praise, blame, and every other word in the English language. The Soul won't give in to any offer. It doesn't want to control nature by obeying. It will beat nature by giving up the body and getting to know itself. Find yourself without a body. When you feel power, it's in your soul and in nature. "We need to break the law and become criminals."

"Deliver thou thyself, by thyself
Ah, do not let thyself sink
For thou art thyself thy greatest friend
And thyself (the relative 'I') thy greatest enemy."

This is not the crazy thoughts of a crazy person, kid. It's the key to SAT-CHIT-ANANDA, which means eternal life, understanding, and happiness. When you reach completeness, you have complete freedom. Would you or do you know what life is all about? To find Sat-chit-ananda is what it sounds like. Man, on the other hand, is trying to find this Perfect Existence in the changing things of this world. If a person knows that the only way to reach the Impersonal Ideal is to give up the things of the "world, the flesh, and the devil" and live by the Impersonal Ideal, then Maya will have done its job, which is to show people their divinity. "Get rid of the desire to live. Get rid of Ambition. Get rid of the need for safety, but work like you love life. Honour life as those who are driven. "Be as happy as people who live to be happy."

In the Light on the Path, Mabel Collins says this. Yes, you should work hard all the time, train your mind, and grow as a person. But don't do these things for yourself; do them for your Higher Self, The BRAHMAN, Eternal to show itself through. If you lose this point of view, all of your personal goals will end in pain and disappointment. You should work just as hard as the eager man and the pleasure-seeking man, but keep in mind that your actions are driven by different things. Spirit is in charge here.

Gema says, "To the work you have the right, O Partha, but not to the fruits thereof." Holding on to success can only lead to decline. The soul shouldn't hold on to anything. The Higher Self must be the focus of all work and effort. You are only honouring your lower self when you care about the results. This is why unselfish work is important. It clears the mind of maya and frees it from its spell, allowing the personal to become impersonal. If you say “I am you, O Lord!” you will destroy the lower “I” forever. If you say “I am nothing, O Eternal One! you are everything!” you will lose the lower “I” and gain the higher one. The first one is for the Gnani and the second one is for the Bhakti Yogi. They both mean the same thing. Love everyone, but don’t count on anyone else’s love. Give everything you have. Don’t take anything. Serve all of them. Do not care about being thanked and served in return. You are the One who will rule forever. There is a lot of power behind you. But you will stay a beggar as long as you are one. Give up the lower self and live for the higher self. What you call “Universal Love” is the lower level representation of receiving ABSOLUTE UNITY on the Buddha level and in Samadhi (Final Enlightenment).

Chapter 7
Somaesthetics and Yoga

Introduction

Somaesthetics is a project by pragmatists that focuses on the body to promote a new view of the "body" as the place where experiences happen and where people appreciate the senses and make themselves look good. The study is critical and positive about the body, how it is used, and what it feels like. It blurs the lines between philosophy, art, and education. In the sense of a "philosophical way of life" and the "art of living," somaesthetics brings out the main goal of philosophy. Somaesthetics needs to be "embodied" in the real world because "practice" is one of its most important parts. Education is a good place for this to happen. The use of practical somathetics in education also gives us a chance to think about the present system of education. This study wants to suggest a new way of looking at education using somaesthetics. I will use my experience with yoga as an example of a new way of teaching that uses somaesthetics.

Richard Shusterman came up with the word "somaesthetics" to go beyond traditional aesthetics, also known as "pragmatist aesthetics," and do more than what analytical aesthetics could do. The first class Shusterman took was in analytic aesthetics, and he used the work of T. S. Eliot as his main source. Eliot's social and cultural views helped him and his "struggle with the limits that define this field [of aesthetics and philosophy]" gave him hope. He also liked John Dewey's "earthy, upbeat, and democratic pragmatism," which is why he "converted" to pragmatism. As pragmatism pushes people to rethink the roles of art and philosophy, Shusterman makes the case that philosophy should be more like real life:

> *Philosophy should be transformational instead of foundational. Rather than a metascience for grounding our current cognitive and cultural activities, it should be cultural criticism that aims to reconstruct our practices and institutions so as to improve the experienced quality of our lives. Improved experience, not originary truth, is the ultimate philosophical goal and criterion.*

Shusterman believed in pragmatist aesthetics, which let him see philosophy and art as ways of life in which the body is an important part "both as a medium of aesthetic self-fashioning and as a means of aesthetic pleasure." Shusterman wants to change the body through somaesthetics. This idea hasn't been talked about much in philosophy and aesthetics writings. Shusterman suggests that somaesthetics has three parts: the analytical, the functional, and the practical. Theoretical philosophy and analysis form the basis of this one-of-a-kind, cross-disciplinary area. What makes it unique is that it also includes the practical side of doing. Because it is useful and melodramatic, somaesthetics can be seen as instruction. The usual way of studying in school tries to figure out the body on a cognitive level, but this "ameliorative study" makes the body (i.e. the somatic self) better. The practical aspect must be included in improvement, along with the written, analytical talk. So, somaesthetics is about the art of living, which can be seen from the point of view of schooling.

The word "education" is often used to refer to the school system, which has many problems and limits. For example, Shusterman doesn't like the way schools work now, and he agrees with Feldenkrais that schools are just a way to make people fit in and lose their sense of who they are. For some reason, it shapes people in many ways, from their bodies and minds to their beliefs. There's also the issue of systematically introducing practical somaesthetics into the school system, like teaching yoga during PE class. This could get rid of the intellectual depth of somaesthetics and reduce the practice to just teaching how to move in a controlled way. Because of this, the word "education" in this chapter doesn't just mean the formal school system and its problems. It's also used to refer to a wider range of things, such as relationships and personal growth.

You can use somaesthetics to get a better sense of this big idea of teaching. "Disciplines of body care provide instead a promising path toward a better public by creating individuals who are healthier and more flexibly open, perceptive, and effective through heightened somatic sensibility and mastery." Which means that the body is an important part of breaking down barriers and growing as a person through better awareness, control, and consciousness. This part doesn't make up a link between somaesthetics and education; instead, it looks at what somaesthetics means for education.

Education through the lens of somaesthetics

Meliorism

Aesthetics is the critical and positive study of the body, and meliorism, or the idea that people can make the world a better place, is also present in education. The main goal of education is to make things better, but this process has many risks in many areas, from the most important parts to the little things that are done every day. But people have tried to find the truth in different ways, such as by using human reason, publicly agreed-upon standards (like the national curriculum), common sense, and the ideas of teachers. The risks depend on how meliorism is identified and used. In real life, the idea of improvement might not fit with the values of both the teacher and the pupil. What does somaesthetics do about these risks related to its meliorism, or desire to make things better?

One of the main ideas behind meliorism in somaesthetics is that we become aware through our bodies. Its goal is to raise one's body awareness, which is why it is sharp and sensitive enough to let one think through it. The meliorism of somaesthetics "should be distinguished from naive, utopian optimism" because becoming more aware of the present is necessary. Somaesthetics knows that the body is connected to both culture and society, so reflection is not being locked up inside the body. Melism in somaesthetics is based on self-reflection and tries to change the body's present state through action.

It is important to keep in mind that any progress requires standards and guidelines, and somaesthetics is not a project that aims to set these standards. Shusterman says that there are different kinds of improvement on many levels, such as a better sense of experience, a more appealing image, or a higher rank in performance. Somaesthetics is a "field of inquiry" that encourages people to think about and explore their senses, movements, feelings, and even the societal norms that they are unconsciously a part of. As things stand, somaesthetics focuses on improving the experiential aspect by doing things like making people more self-aware and adjusting their senses. However, this is just one type of "philosophical toolbox" that can be used to achieve "the critical, reflective art of living".

To-and-fro motion

Meliorism is caused by a back and forth shift between how the body is built and how it feels. Dewey's idea of "experience" talks about this never-ending back and forth between primary and secondary experiences. This idea also goes to the idea of the body in somaesthetics. In the first experience, there are "gross, macroscopic, crude subject-matters." Later, there are "refined, derived objects of reflection" in the second experience. Then it moves on to the main experience. Practicing the back-and-forth motions over and over again leads to a new mode of experience. This is how one can improve and change their experience.

The body of somaesthetics, which is in-between a "background" (like habitual behavior) and a "foreground" (like conscious reflection), can also be thought of in terms of moving back and forth. To get better at some physical behaviors or habits, you need to explicitly think on them to bring them to the forefront of your mind. Because feelings, thoughts, and actions all have physical aspects, the back and forth movement between the body's parts isn't just physical; it may also include the teaching of the somatic self.

Transcendence

To reach transcendence, the body's structures and its perception must move back and forth. This back and forth looking into of body awareness leads the practitioner to a new way of experiencing the body. It's not an absolute truth based on foundationalism or a rejection of the present, limited state in this case:

> *Transcendence, as the urge to reach beyond oneself, may be basic to human existence and is certainly central to pragmatist meliorism, but it need not be interpreted in supernatural terms. Our very being is a flux of becoming*

something else, which can be constructively construed in moral terms of selfimprovement.

According to Shusterman (2002), a player is a good example of someone who should know what they are doing wrong and have the swing to fix it. Once someone knows how their body should feel during a swing, they can't go back to how they were before transcendence. Transcendence doesn't try to change the limited body; instead, it accepts and even faces its limits. This disease isn't just found in athletes, either; it affects more than just the body and includes mental aspects as well. Somaesthetics tries to change the limits between aesthetics and philosophy, which decide what is art and what is true. As an important goal, transcendence (also written as change) can also be applied to the school system. From the point of view of somaesthetics' transcendence, the main conditions of education today, like age, subject, place, and the bond between teacher and student, need to be more adaptable.

Philosophical living: self-cultivation

Somaesthetics is the study of philosophical living, which is closely linked to the question of how one should live. This idea is shared by many Asian fields of self-cultivation, Emerson's Perfectionism, and Dewey's idea of constant "growth." These ideas are about how to make your own style, which can be seen as the teaching goal. To reach a state of transcendence and meliorism, philosophical living involves moving back and forth between different states of awareness and experience. This is not a presentation of a fully formed life; rather, it is a process of developing a style or way of living.

Shusterman talks about Emerson's idea of style, especially how to make your own lifestyle through self-styling, self-creation, and self-culture. He says that the styles are based on the "somatic style," which means that they include more than just sight and sound. They also include action, self-understanding, movement, and emotion. Shusterman says that self-cultivation is "an individual moral injunction to strive to be better and do so by being always open to exploring the claims of different ends." This idea comes from Emerson's idea of perfectionism. These conclusions are a "unattained yet attainable self", but because it happens in steps, attainment is never full. Philosophical living is based on appealing "different life-exemplars", not on common ways to make life better. Somaesthetics shows that the process of making a lifestyle includes the aesthetic process.

Somaesthetics through Yoga

This chapter tries to rethink education from the point of view of somaesthetics using four words: meliorism, to-and-fro motion, transcendence, and philosophical life as self-cultivation. This way of learning is known as "education as a practice in somaesthetics," and it's where people can find somaesthetics and use it to make their own way of life. It's not limited to the current school structure, which includes a regular school, subjects, and teacher-student relationships. Instead, it can be thought of as any physical experience. But just because every physical experience can be seen as a learning tool doesn't mean that every move you take every day is a learning experience. I'm trying to show that education is a practice in somaticism with these four terms. I also look at what "yoga" and "embodied meta-cognitive verbalization" mean based on my practical experience. However, this is only used as an example and is not meant to suggest or promote yoga as a way to practice somaesthetics.

Yoga is a group of widely accepted therapies, practices, and disciplines for physical, mental, and spiritual reasons. Its roots can be traced back to ancient India, but it has changed a lot over the years. One of the most important modern yoga teachers is B.K.S. Iyengar, Evans, and Abrams (2006). He brought yoga to the West. Based on Indian traditional theory, he talks about yoga in many different and deep ways in his book Light on Life. In yoga, there are five layers of the body, which are called kosas. This exercise can help you reach all five layers: the physical, the energetic, the mental, the intellectual, and the divine. People think of yoga as an eight-step process that includes more than just asana and pranayama (posture and breathing). It also includes lessons on how to be moral, meditate, and become enlightened. Hatha yoga is the most popular type of yoga today. It has three goals that can be tracked back to writing from the 14th century to the 17th century:

(1) the total purification of the body, (2) the complete balancing of the physical, mental, and energetic fields, and (3) the awakening of purer consciousness through which one ultimately connects with the divine by engaging in practices rooted in the physical body.

The many different aspects of yoga can be backed up by evidence. Many practitioners don't just want better physical health; they also want better mental health or spiritual freedom. They see yoga as a form of therapy that helps them learn more about themselves and how to manage their feelings and thoughts.

In this study, the method of "embodied meta-cognitive verbalization" was used to practice yoga through somaesthetics. This is a way that Japanese cognitive scientist Masaki Suwa says you can gain "embodied knowledge." A Japanese information scientist named Nishigaki (2018) says that the difference between "absolute theoretical knowledge," which is what traditional science tries to find, and "life knowledge" is a big problem in cognitive science, especially when it comes to studying AI. So-called objective scientific methods make it hard to explain the features of life knowledge, like knowledge that is empirical, heuristic, embodied, unspoken, and situated. However, this is how Suwa is trying to show embodied knowledge. According to Suwa (2008), "it might be impossible to verbalize all that our own body knows and can do." This is because "it is believed that our body knows more than we can verbalize" when it comes to embodied knowledge, like how to play sports or an instrument. But he says that it is important to express and think about embodied knowledge through words (i.e. to verbalize it), analyze it, and make it better, even though verbalization can't fully explain it.

To get embodied knowledge, embodied meta-cognitive verbalization means doing a task and thinking about it over a long period of time (six months or more) and doing it regularly. This known through action is recorded by the artist, and the collection of these records is then studied. Suwa studies embodied knowledge in his lab. This type of knowledge includes a lot of different physical events, like sports, bowling, darts, fashion coordination, walking, tasting, and learning in the classroom. As these bodily experiences are performed over and over, and later, the performers think about them. Suwa says that "reflecting" basically has two parts in this case:

> *'(1) self-awareness of what we think, what we perceive, and how we move our body, and (2) thereby verbalization of them'. Therefore, embodied meta-cognitive verbalisation, which is a first- person perspective method, is not only used for clarification, but it also helps develop embodied knowledge.*

The embodied meta-cognitive verbalisation of yoga: my personal journey

Outline

On this journey, you will do yoga and use the embodied meta-cognitive verbalization way to understand it. I look at yoga's features, meaning, and other aspects to show how it can be used as an example of teaching through somaesthetics. For the yoga practice, the main set of Ashtanga Vinyasa yoga was done about twice a week, and it was accompanied by 80 minutes of video instructions. Based on my own experience with yoga, this style was picked because it was hard for me. It also helps to do the same thing over and over again because it's hard to tell how much progress you are making with yoga from numbers alone. Embodied meta-cognitive verbalization was used to record this yoga exercise. According to Suwa's rules (below), the topics were mostly about how the person felt and what they thought about their body:

- what one thinks or thought
- how one moves or moved body parts
- what one perceives from the environment through five senses, and
- the sense of our body through the proprioceptive system.

The "yoga diary" is made up of twenty-two entries. This will go on for about four months, from April to August 2019, but it is still going on.

The 'Yoga Diary'

There are no rules about how to format a yoga diary

because it's just about writing down your thoughts and feelings about the practice, such as difficult poses, better poses, body sensations, how the body is used in general, and breathing methods. There are three main themes that have come up in all twenty-two yoga diaries so far: poses, feeling things in the body, and breathing. I read the yoga journal again and picked out lines that fit with each theme. All together, there were 213, 260, and 84 sentences for each theme. Some of the sentences crossed over between subjects. Attaching "point tags" to each sentence helped people understand the main idea of the text. This doesn't mean putting things into a number or mechanical category. Instead, it's a way to figure out what the description means, how it fits in with other descriptions, and what the practice is like. The point tags for each subject are shown in Table 1.

Table 1. Three themes of the 'yoga diary' with point tags.

Posing (The number of relevant sentences)	
Sense of improving on a pose (45) Sense of the body in a pose (31) Using the body in an incorrect pose (30) Incorrect pose (22)	Sense of achievement through a pose (6) Thoughts on Ashtanga Vinyasa yoga (6) Evaluation of another's pose (5)
Attempts to improve an incorrect pose (16) Awareness of using the body to improve a pose (12)	Difficulty improving a pose (4) Fatigue when posing (4) Breathing through a pose (4)
Evaluation of overall practice (9)	Joy through a pose (3)
Relationship between pose and breathing (7)	Concentration during practice (2) Feeling relaxed during a pose (2) Gaze while posing (2)

Bodily sensation	
Overall sense of the body (31) Sense of the body when posing (31) Having a kinaesthetic sense while posing (29) Body part that is difficult to be conscious of (27) Sense of body when improving pose (26) Kinaesthetic sense when attempting to improve a pose (20) Sense of body by comparing to others (19) Connecting the breath and body (17)	Sense of weakness that is preventing a pose (12) Vision when posing (7) Developing a sense of the body (6) Past bodily experience (5) Connecting awareness and movement (2) Attempting body awareness (3) Sense of body after posing (2) Sense of body preventing a pose (2) Auditory sensation when posing (1) Sense of body when breathing (1)
Breathing	
Controlling breathing quality (18) Awareness of various breathing qualities (15) Instructions and breathing (13) Awareness of body sensation through breathing (10) Connecting breathing and movement (9) Difficulty controlling breathing quality (5)	Changing body awareness through breathing (4) Improving poses through breathing (4) Being out of breath (3) Breathing and vision (2) Relationship between breathing and concentration (2) Posing in a way that is likely to improve breathing awareness (1)

The meaning of 'Proficiency'

The yoga journals show that the person who does the yoga always wants to feel more "proficient" in it. "Proficiency" in this case means getting better at bad poses and doing a pose well. But it's not clear what a "good pose" in yoga means because it's not measured or scored. But the goal is to get as close as possible to the pose that is shown. A practitioner writes in their diary on April 23: "I feel that my hips are slightly higher and support the ground only by my arm, compared to the person in the video who makes the body parallel to the ground during chaturanga dandasana pose." Comparing yourself to the model to find your weaknesses is an example of getting better at something.

What does "proficient" mean in the diaries? It can be found in the themes of "posing" and "body sensation," especially in the point tags "sense of improving on a pose" and "awareness of using the body to improve a pose." There are different meanings for "proficiency" in the lines that use these point tags:

> *... change in the sense of the back, vitality, feeling of using the back, deepening of sensation, lifting easily and lightly, lightness, quietly carrying legs, control, speed control, easy to feel the weight, jump lightly like skipping, supporting weight, arm fatigue, reduced body tremor, stability, weight distribution, height of leg, significant irritation around the pelvis, stretching on the upper body, keeping balance, sharp pain in the left scapula, pain due to relieving the stiffness, stamina remaining ...*

Instead of trying to make the perfect example, practitioners focus on the body and kinesthetic senses that they are already aware of. For instance, when they talked about skill, they talked about pain, tiredness, or other major irritations. In yoga, which includes doing the same poses over and over, the practitioner gets better by learning new body senses and improving the way they move.

In particular, getting a sense of the body, or the practitioner's "back," seems to be the main meaning of competence. Point tags that say "body part that is difficult to be conscious of" in the theme "bodily sensation" show that the back, lower abdomen, and scapula are often mentioned as these parts of the body. In the yoga notebook, the back is shown like this:

... unable to use power, unnecessary flesh, the unknown area where consciousness does not reach, unpleasant feeling, heavy, extra, useless, sense of flesh, uncontrollable, chunks of flesh, hard, vast undeveloped, how to be conscious of it is unknown ...

Because the back makes you feel uncomfortable, which is part of your mind and sense of control, yoga tries to make you more aware of this. The first sentence of the point tag that said "developing a sense of the body" talked about how awareness didn't get to this part. They worked hard, though, to control these areas by directing their feelings and actions.

The idea of "breathing" can also be seen as proficiency, which means learning and getting better at feeling things. From April to May, the first step was to match your breathing to the video's directions. From May to August, the next step was to become more aware of the different ways you breathe. In the journals, the following breathing traits were written down:

... exaggerated breathing, regular breathing, evenly regulated breathing, breathing out and breathing in rapidly, blocked breath, breathing in a vacuum state, breath out like spitting as the moment of over lifting, breathing like a sigh, breath that makes a noise, breath that rubs the vocal cords, normal transparent breath, breath sucking with the mouth, breath with a constant rhythm, breathing that self-controlled . . .

The conscious attempt to explore and control these different aspects of the breath has been improved. The stomach, spine, ribs, lower abdomen, throat, torso, and ribcage were also mentioned as parts of the body.

Using embodied meta-cognition verbalization, yoga practitioners' accounts of what "proficiency" meant to them were looked at. Most of the ideas that people had about this subject were related to the question of why they did yoga in the first place. They didn't see "proficiency" as getting close to the perfect pose; instead, they wanted to feel their bodies in new ways every time they practiced.

Shifting issues

In each entry of the yoga diary, two to eight "issues" were brought up. These "issues" included the practitioner's needs for growth, thoughts, and questions. Ten problems were found that showed up in two or more notebook entries. These problems weren't known before practice; they were found in the yoga journal after the fact. The ten issues below can be broken down even further into four themes: "pose," "body," "breath," and "concentration."

Pose: (1) chaturanga dandasana, (2) maricyasana, (3) sirsasana, (4) bending forward

Bodily sensation: (5) weakness in the lower abdomen, (6) relationship between body consciousness and movement

Breath: (7) instruction and breathing, (8) quality of breathing

Concentration: (9) length of time, (10) concentration

Figure 1 displays how these problems change over time. In this case, the problem of "(9) length of time" changed to "(10) concentration." The fact that practitioners said the 80-minute class was long and boring in April shows that they were having some trouble focusing. But in June, the problem became clearly a "(10) concentration" problem. In order to focus on body awareness, they tried to separate themselves from new distractions. The problem with "(7) instruction and breathing" changed into a problem with "(8) quality of breathing." They were trying to align their breathing with the directions, but now they were also trying to improve their own breathing.

Figure 1. Ten shifting issues in the 'yoga diary'.

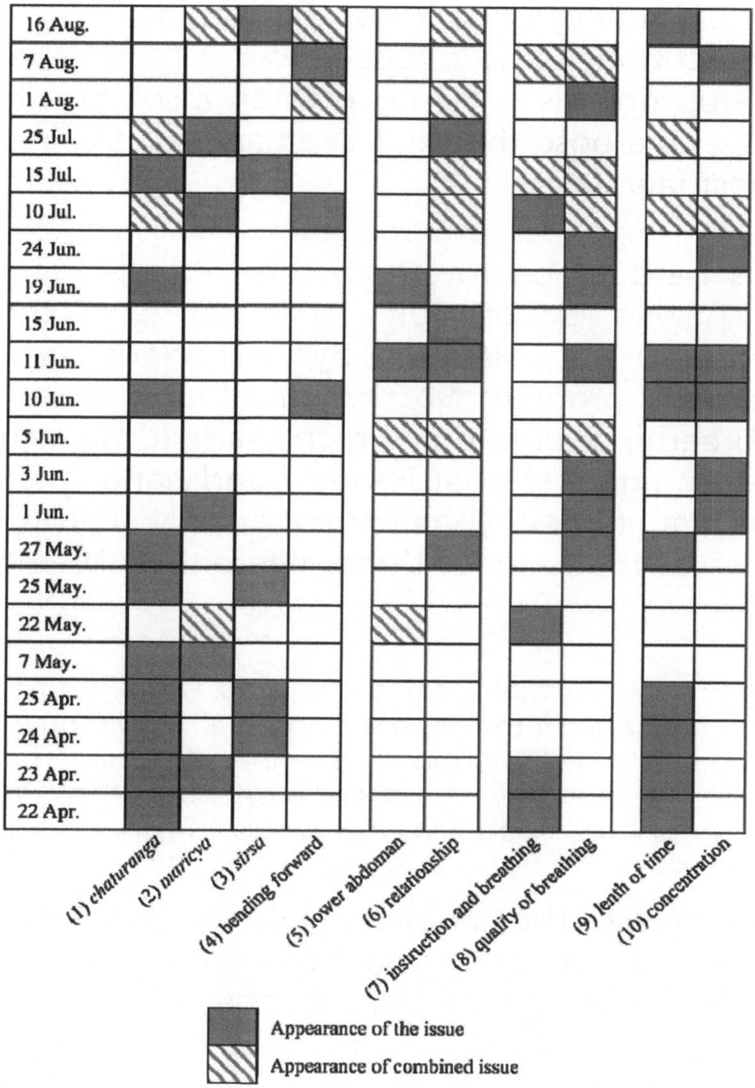

Sometimes, issues would also combine, which is what the striped squares on the table represent (i.e. two or more combined issues). On May 22, for example, the issues of '(2) maricyasana' and '(5) weakness of the lower abdomen' had combined to create the new issue of 'maricyasana/lower abdominal weakness'. The practitioner also noticed how a new issue that appeared on this day may provide a solution to the maricyasana pose that had been an ongoing issue for the past few weeks.

It was hard to be aware of the "ribcage" problem that showed up on July 10 in terms of the "(6) relationship between body consciousness and movement" problem. So, these problems joined with the "breathing" problem, which made it mix with the long-standing "(1) chaturanga dandasana" problem. In the practitioner's yoga journal on July 10, this issue, which was made up of three different problems, was written:

> *When I lower the ribcage to the ground, I lower and at the same time push it toward the front as if I am lifting it, the ribcage not the chest, and then connect to urdhvamukha svanasana pose. Then, the pose became tightened up and stability increased.*

It seemed like the problem with the pose was with the ribs instead of the chest when you had to try to move while being aware of the "chest."

To sum up, the practitioner's tasks were constantly moved, combined, and changed during the practice time. This made the body move back and forth between the background and the foreground. If you question an action, set tasks, and look for ways to make it better, you are thinking about more than just your yoga practice. You are thinking about both the practice and the discipline. Repeating the yoga exercise over and over and using the meta-cognitive method to help with reflection may have changed the practice.

Final considerations

As an example of how somaesthetics can be used in real life, a yoga practice that uses an embodied meta-cognition verbalization method was looked at. This part gave a broad picture of education as the ongoing search for change that leads to a better state of life. Somaesthetics says that growth is an aesthetic process that involves making a way of life instead of an ethical rule. To put it another way, pushing oneself to new heights and learning more about how to improve oneself are always part of the curriculum. In this way, thinking of somaesthetics as a form of education might help you understand other ideas and events that have to do with education. Because of this, it should be possible to look at the present education system from a different angle. It might be possible to use "education as a practice in somaesthetics" in a way that approaches "mathematics" or "sports education," for instance. For a long-term view of the school system, this is a good idea. Somaesthetics says that the first step to growth is becoming more aware of your body and the back and forth movement between your body and your experiences, changes, and philosophical living as self-cultivation. "Education as a Practice in

Somaesthetics" refers to these important points of view for education.

As a performative somatic experience and teaching tool, sports are a good way to practice somaesthetics because they let you change unhealthy habits like bad posture and movement. A somaesthetic reflective sports practice can include more than just movements. It can also include emotions and feelings like passion, excitement, pleasure, and sadness. So, it can lead to philosophy, which means asking things like, "Why am I doing this?" or "What does it mean to play sports?" This kind of thinking helps us see things from outside of sports and shape our style from a bigger picture point of view.

Somaesthetics says that a sport is already a practice because the players are always trying to change, which usually happens during workouts instead of games. Internal tasks are set up freely in order to get better in a way that is dynamic and includes both practice and constant, circular change. A person will be kinaesthetically aware while they train and pay attention to their stance and how their body feels. It's important for athletes to know that sports aren't just about playing on the field. They're also about other things in their lives, like lifting weights, going down the street, watching videos, reading books, having conversations, and learning. Movements that are slow and still, like those in yoga, zazen, and the Feldenkrais method, can help motivate you to do these things.

Even though the practice is still going on, I looked into what the practitioner meant when they talked about feeling "proficient" and how they saw the tasks that were changing over time in their yoga practice. A lot of things from the past, like the advice of my past teachers, yoga books, the classes I teach, magazines, and videos, helped me think about myself for this part. "Education as a practice in somaesthetics" may not come from just doing yoga. Instead, it comes from being aware of your current bodily experience, which includes past relationships, the never-ending desire to get better, and the process of making a self-style through these efforts.

Chapter 8
Self-Master

Introduction

In Previous Chapters, we introduced you to the mysteries of Will and Mind-Force, as well as the laws that guide the universe and how things grow. We have also shown you how to gain complete power over your mind and body. Through these lessons, we've tried to show you how to have the right "Mental Attitude" about your daily life, so that while you're focusing on self-cultivation, you can also help strengthen the race. On top of that, our convictions, beliefs, and ideals are not small parts of what determines our health and the world we live in. They respond to our situations and to the WHOLE MAN. We have also taught you important things about Soul Unfoldment, Meditation, Bramhacharya, Breathing, Fasting, Health-Culture, Body Building, and we have shown you, as clearly as we could, the exact steps you need to take to develop one virtue. This way, you can learn how to develop other virtues as well, since the steps and thoughts are very similar and focus on the most important ones. In terms of how the body and soul grow, evolve, and unfold, we have given you the bare body of truth, removing the metaphysical wrappings and theoretical draperies that they are dressed in. In order to get to the divine face of truth, we had to physically rip the heavy wheel apart. That's why our lessons are short and to the point. There was another big problem that we had to deal with and solve. These amazing mystic truths lose some of the deep seriousness and holiness that is present in Sanskrit literature when they are written in our everyday English language. But a smart and thoughtful student—and we don't write for silly and careless people—won't let the fact that they seem simple fool or catch them off guard. He should instead understand that these lessons can be used in any way and in any part of life. Just put them into action, and he'll see right away how they can help him in his daily life. Not the "WHAT" of things, but the "HOW" of them all. We let each kid figure out how to solve the intellectual side of the ETERNAL PROBLEM in his own way. To sum up, we need to say that this Course doesn't even try to cover the more advanced steps of yoga in full. But they will definitely get him ready for those greater things by taking away the PALL OF DARKNESS from his mind.

There must be a lot of you for whom the "Fearless" mind is not only something to envy but also something you have never experienced. Being honest with other people might hurt your pride, so you might not say it, but deep down inside you, you really want to be a Fearless Individual. And it's a good thing to want. In order to see Heavenly Joy and Superhuman Strength, you must be able to wipe away all fear, anxiety, and worry from your mind. This is not an easy job. And I tell you all, you can be fearless. You can be anything you want to be. I've seen it. It's done. In this paper, I will give you good advice that will help you push forward towards your goal. The psychological basis for these directions is sound, and they have been tried and tested by millions of people. They have been a blessing to everyone who followed them with all their heart. If you want to be Fearless, don't think twice about following them to the letter.

I won't waste time telling you about how bad it is to be afraid, be cowardly, worry, be anxious, or have a lot of bad thoughts that come from fear. Man is what he thinks in his heart, in his body, in his mind, and in his spirit. You are what you think you are. Mind controls and either makes or breaks everything, in the real world and in other worlds. Your thoughts have an effect on your health, your situations, and the people around you, including those who are close to you, those who are far away, and even those who you think of as "dead" but are actually alive in spirit and connected to you through thought and soul. Every minute, they affect you and are affected by you. A man's daily thoughts have a huge impact on many areas of his life. It is taken in by trees, animals, rocks, and other things that are made of matter. Thought-force is leaving its mark on the walls of your room, the clothes you wear, and the letters you write. A clairvoyant or psychometerist can read your mind by looking at a letter, a lock of hair, a piece of cloth, or anything else that has to do with one of your friends. They will then use their psychic abilities to figure out that person's appearance, personality, past and present history, and anything else that is connected to that person. Wonderful, "Impossible!" you exclaim in shock. It's done now, though. Through study and research, you can learn how important your thoughts are and keep them pure by staying away from fearful, angry, sexual, and vain ideas. That's right, these four huge weeds are poisonous to the Tree of Life's roots. Because of these four bad ideas and their millions of offspring, everyone in the world is in pain in different ways. You may say this is all good, but:

HOW?

That is just what I mean to teach you all along. I don't want to feed you on mere empty theories, but I can and I will give you that knowledge which when assimilated shall build up strong flesh, bone, muscle, tissue, pith and marrow which will give you superb health, strength of mind and spirit--all of which are necessary adjuncts to Spiritual Growth and Happiness. Let me give you in detail methods and exercises. The ideal fearless man has many qualities. I say the Ideal Hero--no imitation patch work vulgarian. These qualities are in rough detail: (1) Devotion to God. (2) Knowledge. (3) Concentration. (4) Will Power. (5) Energy and Aspiration. (6) Health. (7) Self-Esteem. (8) Self-Control. (9) Love for Humanity. (10) Chastity. There may be other qualities but you will do well to build up the above and others will come to you by themselves. Let me drop a few helpful suggestions on the above.

Follow each sentence closely.

1. Devotion to the Absolute Will

I have always thought, written, noticed, and felt that people who are devoted to God are the bravest. Men like that are hard to find. Yes, you all fully understand what "Fearlessness" means. It means complete freedom; to put it another way, he is the FEARLESS man who "fears-nothing" and "faces-everything." Everyone is part of that everything. That doesn't leave anyone out. From this point of view, isn't the brave man something you don't see very often? You may come across different levels of confidence. Now, a person with this trait to the "highest degree" believes in this God. Each person has their own idea of God. Each person has their own unique view of the absolute. What you believe about God will work for you. It will work for you and you alone, I say. Don't make other people do it. Do not share it with anyone. Want a better idea of God? Say this prayer in silence: "O, Thou, I do not understand your nature." I DO NOT KNOW, BUT I WANT TO KNOW. Do you show yourself to my soul? "Open my spiritual eyes and lead me on." Please, student, don't take this lightly. Do not pay attention to your proud or blind brother who says he doesn't care about God and can get by without God's help. Do not listen. Do not listen. The strongest and best people pray a lot. But they don't tell other people about this. They never show how much they love each other. They have all prayed, though, and they still do. Not only do they believe in hard work, but they also believe in divine direction and leading. Get used to being "led by the Spirit." This is how everything will work out for you. You will also see that the Fearless guy is not just a guy who fears God. He is a person who loves God. He mostly loves God because God is God. A fake believer is someone who is afraid even though they love God. But the kindness of the LORD'S name is so great that it can clean up even the dirtiest heart. It will turn even a fake devotee into a real one, and over time, that real devotee will be able to do anything. Trust in God because of this. "Be regular" in your prayers. Also, keep in mind that every trial is a pain that comes with spiritual renewal; every pain is a way to make the herald of a glorious dawn of knowledge stronger. So stop getting upset. The great God, whose infinite power controls the movements of planets and keeps track of the fall of a sparrow, wants what's best for your life. It is His will that you do everything, say everything, feel everything, hope everything, and have everything. What people want is what God wants. What God wants is what people want. And who can explain God? God is the only one who can describe Himself. He has said that He is the Universe, or Brahman. For a person who loves God, nothing is impossible. He only needs to be ready to work, and God will take care of everything else. Regular devotion to God will definitely make you very fearless. "Love is God."

2. Knowledge (Gnayanam)

Fear is due to ignorance. When in the dark of night you mistook the rope for a snake, you shrieked out in terror. Cause? IGNORANCE. But when you saw the rope as a rope, you laughed out in amusement. Cause? KNOWLEDGE.

All your fear is due to your ignorance of your real nature. All the fear at the last is fear of death. You have to realise through knowledge of the Vedanta that you are birthless, deathless. You have to unfold by meditation a consciousness of your Real Self. I give you hereunder a meditation exercise that will help you in this direction.

Meditation Exercise 1

Take a break in the SILENCE. Turn off all thoughts and plans that have to do with the outside world. Consider that you, the Real Ego, are not the body. The body is just a garment you wear to work on the physical plane, and you will take it off one day. Believe that you will live forever and that even if a thousand bodies come and go, you, the Ego, will still be living. These are your identities, or shadows. What dies and what is born is just a fantasy, a dream that you make real for certain reasons. All of these goals are centred on one POTENTIALIZED GOAL: to take over matter.

This means you, the Ego, live in the Supernal Regions, on the spiritual plane, with your Father in Heaven. But you have come down to matter to find the most objective statement possible. Understand that you, the Ego, are a separate part of the Great Consciousness and that you are THE ABSOLUTE EGO SUM of the whole universe and all of its big and small forms. You have all of the powers and qualities of the Absolute

Self. Realise that you are not the feelings and passions that come out in your personality. It is up to the law of flux and rhythm to control these things. Reason and will are the regulating and equalising forces of mind. See that you are not the mind or the intellect; you are just using these parts of yourself to study and examine the outside effects of nature. Realise that you are pure Consciousness, Bliss, and Existence at your core. Join the flow of life. Realise that the form part of manifestation is just your mind concentrating and forming things. Your subjective nature is the same as the subjective selves of other people. It is a way for the GREAT SUBCONSCIOUS to come in and go out. Realise your unity with all living things, which shows itself objectively as the brotherhood of all living things and the perfect recognition of the All-Father-Mother, also known as God, who is the Great Cosmic Power and Intelligence. God's intelligence, all-bliss, and existence are always pouring into each Unit of Individualised Divine Energy and changing through nature. As a student, if you meditate every day on the fact that you are not your body, your emotions, or your mind, you will awaken the "I am I" awareness that guides your personality. This is what has been called Soul-awareness. After that, you will be spiritually awake to Chaitanya. After that, you won't feel any fear. Fear will fall away like an old covering. All fears come from a race consciousness that hasn't fully formed yet. This race consciousness affects each person's consciousness and is stamped on almost every atom of matter. Because you believe you are the body, you "fear." If you truly understand that you have the power to control as many bodies as you desire, that you are a spiritual being expressing and energising through physical bodies, and that you will never die, then fear will be afraid of you and stop tormenting and kidding you. Fear lives in the matter-fed mind, which is the mind that has grown up by taking in and responding to outside feelings and stimuli. This mind is also known as the objective mind. This mind sees itself in the form, in the body. It is set on the form-side, the concrete side of reality and can't be stopped. The forces of Maya make it dark, and all it can see is the body. Being apart is all it sees. Yes, it is the mind that is given matter. People who have developed this part of their awareness are always selfish, have small, cone-shaped eyes, and only care about their own well-being. They can be scared and enjoy making other people afraid of them. The soul, the Subjective Man, or the "I am I" part of consciousness needs to shine light on this thought. Minds that are fed on matter think that you are both a body and a soul. This is not true. You are both a soul and a body. When Soul Consciousness comes into being, a person becomes a Force for good. He doesn't have any fears. His voice is strong, but it doesn't crush and control. Instead, it fills cold and hopeless hearts with warmth, life, energy, hope, and unbreakable courage. It's something that some people are born with. Do not think that I am feeding the ideas of eccentricity. When a boy played with other kids, I often asked myself, "Are you the same person who is running, jumping, and shouting?" I would stop and stare straight ahead. Something would make me feel lost, and I would forget everything. I could clearly and vividly remember how I felt. I get it now. Soul-Consciousness played out in a past life and was fighting for "recognition" in this life. These men are calm when they think about DEATH. They know they can't die. These kinds of men can't hate for a long time. They also have their own physical traits and signs that set them apart. They show a higher level of intelligence. Finally, when you fully understand everything, your only goal in life will be to give other people the same sense of freedom you have. You won't be able to laugh and smile while your brother-man is in pain or doesn't know he's flawed. You will understand what it means to "feel" for people and even animals. In some ways, you will get a sense of the deep pain that the Buddhas, Christs, Ramakrishnas, and Vivekanandas felt. They were hurt, and they felt sorry for people. And when weak humanity put them on the cross, they did it with the same kind of strength that a nurse uses to take the hits and abuse from a sick patient. "Father, forgive them; they do not know what they are doing." Really, to know everything is to forgive everything. You have the same Soul-Consciousness as everyone else. For those who meditate on the Infinite and the Formless Absolute—the Over-soul of the universe—they find it. This is the Brahman of Vedanta, the Self of thinkers, the Atman of yogis, the personal and impersonal God of devotees, and finally, the humanity of humanitarians.

Concentration

Mind can only think of one thing. Worry is the long-term form of negative focus, while fear is the short-term form. If you can focus on one thing and block out or "shut off" all other ideas, fear and worry will not be able to control you. Many of the things you worry about never come true, and others can be stopped by a strong front. No matter what bad things happen to you, you have the strength to "bear up" bravely. As a thought habit, fear is just something bad. There is a bad habit in the mind. Having a positive attitude of Courage is the best way to get rid of this weed from your thoughts. While you think certain things, certain groups of brain cells are either being made or destroyed. Making more positive brain cells is the best way to get rid of negative brain cells. Do not fight your fear feelings if you want to get rid of them. It's like trying to figure out how dark a place is and then throwing it out by the bag. You are aware that you can't do it. The room will be filled with light as soon as you open the windows and let the sun in. A psychologist once said that bad thoughts can make your mind feel like a dirty washbowl full of dirty water. Place the bowl of water near a tap and turn it on. Soon, the steady flow of clean water will get rid of all the dirty water and fill the bowl with clear water. Getting rid of bad thoughts is only possible by having a steady flow of good ones. To get rid of fear thoughts, you should think thoughts of courage. Do not lie on your stomach and do not beg Heaven to see what a disgusting thing you are. No, no, no, no. Be brave. Think about bravery. Tell them to be brave. That's how it works. Face the rising sun. Choose "Courage" as your word. Say it out loud as much as you can. Keep it in your mind deep and strong. You should always tell yourself that you are brave, day or night. Never tell yourself that you are weak.

Now, you need to have CONCENTRATION to stop having fearful thoughts and start having courageous ones. You should be able to change your mind about anything you want. Does that sound like what you mean? I remember reading something about Napoleon that I'd like to say in my own words. While he was sick and on St. Helena and being punished, his doctor asked him one day what the secret was to his amazing success and power. Napoleon told the doctor, "Doctor, my brain is full of chests." I open the "Politics" drawer when I want to think about politics, the "Law" drawer when I want to think about Josephine, and so on. When I close all of these drawers, I can go to sleep. The doctor gave a dull smile of disbelief. "Doctor, I can show you right now. Doctor, I closed all the drawers." As he said this, Napoleon hit his pillow hard. He was sound asleep. The man of science and medicine looked at him in every way, but Napoleon was already sound asleep. Concentration and Mind-Control are what this is. I don't like guys like Napoleon who are selfish. They belong in dark hell. They feed on other people with their power. I don't deny, though, that he had great mental skills. Napoleon was a great Yogi in a past life, but the bad Karma he carried around with him and the effects of his past life led to the terrible events in his career that you all know about. There's no question that God only used this man to bring about certain changes and revolutions.

Pay attention to the things you do every day to improve your concentration. Don't forget about little things.

Pay close attention to everything you do, say, or think. Keep your eyes open, man. Do not do your work while half asleep. Show some signs of life and wake up. Move forward. Think a lot and right to the point.

Will-Power

You all understand this. It is that aspect of your make-up that enables you to make your mind and body obey you. The true principle of Will is closely interlocked with the "I am I" as I have already explained it.

Resolve at the start to do one thing once in 24 hours that you would do if you were not afraid. Face fear and it is your slave. Your Will-power enables you to prove things practically to yourself and to the world; to make actions match-thoughts. Give your Will much exercise in the right direction. Without Will a man is no better than a log of wood. Keep your Will strong by auto-suggestion and exercise. Try the powers of your Will on your personality till you can do anything and be anything. Say "I can and I will" in a thousand different ways and prove it too. The requisite qualities that form valuable adjuncts to Will-power are:

1. Determination. 2. Stick-to-itiveness. 3. Perseverance. 4. Invincible and indomitable courage. 5. Non-attachment. 6. Faith in yourself. 7. Faith in God. 8. I can and I will. Repeat this affirmation often till it becomes a constant mental trait.

Affirmations

I. I am fearless. I am full of courage. There is nothing to fear. I say courage, I think, I act courage.

II. Courage is my distinct and leading trait. Everyone knows me

III. as a man of Indomitable courage. The criticisms and opinions of others cannot affect me the least.

IV. I am part of the Divine Self. I harm none. My nature knows no harm. Hence no harm comes to me.

V. I am equal to anything. Nothing can crush my spirit. I can face everything. I can face everybody.

VI. My powers of resistance are strong, strong, strong. I use them never for the aggression of others. They are for my self-defence.

VII. I am absolutely fearless morally and physically.

VIII. I stand for absolute truthfulness and justice and manifest them in myself.

IX. Work with this affirmation. Strongly implant it in your mind. The use of strong, positive Affirmation in the Silence is valuable in that it gives you a firm hold of your thought so that you can "carry the thought" mentally. The value of expressing thought in act and speech lies in this that it clinches your thought into a permanent habit. Remember this psychologic axiom: 1. Thoughts take form in action. 2. Action induces thought and corresponding habits. Therefore act out the part physically. If you want a courageous mind--"act out" the part physically, in your daily life, on suitable occasions, in all earnestness as you would in a theatre or drama. In a very short time it shall become a confirmed habit. Force yourself to it. Take an interest in what you do and say. Have confident expectations of SUCCESS. Never be daunted and cowed down by initial difficulties and failures. Never say die. If you go down--don't remain lying and moaning. Never, I say, never. Get up. Shake yourself up free and say, like the royal lion "Come one, come all, this rock shall fly sooner from its base than I." Have a will of your own and be a force for good. Exercise your Will-power. Be something. Do something.

Kindness, Vigor, Inspiration, Self-Confidence

It's very important to note the difference between Self-Esteem and Self-Conceit. It's important to me that you fully understand this difference. Self-esteem is definitely a trait of men. It comes from a strong belief that God is King and that Man is the Son. A man is a respectable being with divine qualities. He shouldn't be ashamed of his Creator by lying on the ground. This is having self-esteem. Self-esteem does not go down. It never brings others down. There will never be a boss of people who doesn't have a lot of faith in himself. Again, though, you will never see a real person enjoying making other people fall down in front of them. They are hurt and shocked by what they see. They are humiliated beyond measure by this sorry show. But it's pride in oneself that makes a person make a big deal out of himself. "I am greater than you" is an old, dirty, and manly way to feel. Men like that are hogs, hogs, hogs. Their moms didn't really make them boys. These people are liars and idiots. If you meet this kind of person and have the chance to deal with him on your own, show him how haughty he is. There is some strong stuff in him that he will change. In that case, let him fry in his fat. Nature and its strict rules will teach us a lesson one day. But don't put up with their nonsense because you don't have any morals. That mean and small part of you will be fought against by the "I am" in you. Do not encourage it. Honour God. Respect yourself and other people. Finally, when it comes to energy and ambition, these two traits can change your mind from a negative type to a positive type. It's like they give you a thought force that never knows fear. In fact, fear is dying of lack of food. Move forward. Show that you care about the world's problems and try to make things better. First, raise yourself. Then help other people. Have a life that is becoming more purposeful. Work towards getting it done. When a person gives up the world, they don't become a burden to others. He helps other people take care of their duties. Nature helps people grow into strong people. It always scrapes off barnacles because it doesn't need them. Leeches, vampires, and parasites are not welcome in nature. The goal should be to do something great "for the good of many, for the happiness of many." Live for a reason. Having a positive life purpose will make you feel good and make your thinking positive as well. You will get all-strength. A life with no purpose sets off a lot of negative emotions, including sickness, fear, worry, and other things that break people down. They don't worry the Purposeful Man because he doesn't have time for them. Please understand that faith is not being lazy, no matter what else it is.

Affirmations

I. I have perfect Self-Confidence. I am a Divine Being. I lower not myself--I lower not others.

II. My Life-Purpose is Constructive--not Destructive.

III. I will be great spiritually and mentally. I will make others great. I am an irresistible force for good.

IV. I live to some great purpose. I am an Individual. I recognize the Fatherhood of God and the Brotherhood of man.

Wellness, Purity, and Restraint

Being chaste and self-controlled will help you keep your body clean and healthy. A healthy body means a brain that works well. And having a strong brain means having a lot of energy, charisma, and drive. Remember that our goal is to make people more brave. The Chaste brain has a lot of power. You should follow Bramhacharya, which means keeping the body's vital energy. You need to learn to control your cravings and passions. The energy your body makes shouldn't be taken away at the base of your being. Instead, it should be changed into creative action in your mind and spirit. First, clean up your body. You can get it by not eating or drinking anything and working out.

Fasting and Self-Control

If you feel emotionally sluggish or like your body and mind are heavy, it's a sure sign that your system is "clogged" with waste because the physical channels of elimination aren't working as they should. You have been living a high life and being gluttonous, or you have been enjoying physical pleasures and have worn out your body's important fibres. You may not have drunk enough water, which is what your body needs to clean its vessels. Because you haven't been active much, your body may not have had enough air to burn off carbon and give your blood energy. Having "weak nerves," sadness, hopelessness, fear, trouble focusing, and other mental weaknesses can be caused by too much trash in the system. Here are just a few of the perks that can come from scientific fasting:--(1) It lets nature "clean up." As the saying goes, the day of fasting is like "house cleaning." (2) Just like a galvanic battery, the body "recovers" its power. It is always best to let your digestive system rest after a careful fast. There is no case of dyspepsia, constipation, etc. that can't be helped or completely healed by fasting. Fasting will improve your body's ability to absorb nutrients, make you hungry faster, clean and strengthen your nerves, and improve your health in every way. (3) If you can control your hunger, you can control your lower nature. It's a great way to work on your Will. You will become more spiritually strong. You will become more accepting of your body's wants and needs. Jesus Christ fasted for 40 days to get ready for his big test and temptation. They are all great at going faster.

How to Fast

Do not take on too much. Start with a 24-hour fast if you have never done one before. Drink at least five and, if possible, eight tumblers of clean water slowly and often. Keeping your mind and body gently moving and busy all day is important. You might feel dizzy, like you've lost all your energy, and have a strong desire for food. These are naughty tricks played on an artificial, cultivated, and pampered stomach. Don't give your body anything else besides water. Always remember the difference between the soul, which is the royal "I-am-I," and the body, which is the sensual animal.

During a fast, the most important thing is to think high thoughts and forget about what your body needs. Do not think about your fast. If you do think, tell yourself, "This is to make my will stronger." Take in a lot of fresh air. Walk and do light exercises. For religious reasons, some learned men were afraid to go for a walk during the day "lest they should feel hungry." What a shame! A little hunger is too much to handle! You should take a full bath every day in the morning, fast or not.

Don't be scared. Christ said, "Man does not live by bread alone, but by every word that comes from God's mouth." You might die of hunger, but not from fasting. Deprive all sickness and weakness of their power over you. Your mind controls your body. Make this mental power clear. Lastly, your body is open to what you say when you're fasting. Repeat over and over again that you are brave. Be brave in what you think, what you say, and what you do. Give it some time by the forelock. Right now, force your ideas on your body and mind.

How to Break a Fast

Be sure to keep your reaction in check when you break your fast. Eat very little and only healthy food. Keep your body clean now that it's clean. You can learn to go without food for 40 days straight.

Transmuting Sex-Energy

Here is some sensible advice from a leading thinker and teacher:

To be a perfect Bramhacharin (a regenerate).

1. You must have a clean, healthy body; 2. Good breathing capacity and some control over same; 3. A strong will such as can move body and mind; 4. Assiduous cultivation of the intellectual side; 5. Control over emotions; 6. A fearless mind; 7. Great determination; 8. and abstemious living and high thinking.

The Yogis know a lot about how to use and abuse the reproductive principle in both men and women. It's possible that some hints of this secret knowledge have made it to Western writers who have written about the subject, which has been very helpful. Here in this short book, we can only briefly touch on the topic. Instead of going into theory, we will instead teach a practical breathing exercise that will help the student turn re-productive energy into vitality for the whole system instead of wasting it on lustful indulgence in or out of marriage. The energy used for reproduction is creative energy that can be changed by the system into strength and vitality. This makes it work for regeneration instead of generation. These basic ideas would save many young men in the West a lot of pain and unhappiness in the long run. They would also make them stronger mentally, morally, and physically.

This change in the sexual energy makes the person doing it feel more alive. Some people call this "personal magnetism." They will be filled with a lot of vital force that will spread out from them. The energy that was changed in this way can be put into new pathways and used very effectively. Because its goal is to make things, nature has turned one of its strongest forms of prana into useful energy. The place with the least amount of vital force has the most of it. The reproductive organ is the most powerful storage factory in animals. Its power can be drawn up and used, or it can be used up in the normal processes of reproduction or wasted in wild lust. We can only tell our students the above facts without trying to prove them. Most of our students already know something about the theories of regeneration.

The Yogi exercise for transmuting re-productive energy is simple. It is coupled with rhythmic breathing, and can be easily performed. It may be practised at any time, but is especially recommended when one feels the instinct more strongly, at which time the re-productive energy is manifesting and may be most easily transmuted for regenerative purpose. The exercise is as follows:-

Do not think or imagine about sexual things. Instead, keep your mind on the idea of energy. When these thoughts come up, don't let them get you down. Instead, see them as signs of a force that you want to use to make your body and mind stronger. You can either lie down or sit up straight and focus on the idea of pulling the re-productive energy up to the Solar Plexus. There, it will be changed and stored as a vital energy reserve. Then breathe slowly and steadily, picturing that with each breath you take in you are drawing up new energy. As you breathe in and out, tell your Will to pull energy up from the reproductive system to the solar plexus with each breath. As long as the rhythm is pretty solid and the mental picture is clear, you will be aware of the energy moving up and feel how it stimulates you. You can draw more mental force to your brain instead of the Solar Plexus if you want to. Do this by giving yourself a mental command and picturing the transmission to your brain.

The person who is doing creative work in their mind or body can use this creative energy in their work if they do the above exercise and draw it in with their breath and let it out with their breath. In this last type of exercise, only the parts that are needed for the work will be sent to the work itself. The rest will be stored in the Solar Plexus.

Of course, you'll understand that what is drawn up and used is not the reproductive fluids themselves, but the etheric prana energy that moves them, or the "soul" of the reproductive organism. As part of the transmuting exercise, it is normal to let the head naturally bend forward.

Do this breathing exercise with strength. Be brave. Do not rush as you learn how to do 100 Pranayams at once. When you think a lot and do deep breathing exercises, Will-Culture, regular meditation, and live a clean, normal life, your latent powers will definitely come to life. Don't worry if things move slowly at first.

Keep up your good mood and work slowly. Things will go your way if you don't give up and fight until the end. Have faith in yourself that knows no limits. Finally, keep deep breathing if you want to make more room in your Wisdom and Power. Pranayam is the key to getting spiritually rich. "Spirituality is having enough breath." Almost all types of mental and physical weakness are caused by breathing that isn't smooth or deeply. If you follow these steps and only do the breathing exercise, you will see big results. But to get all the benefits, you need to follow all of these steps regularly and methodically.

The sex-force in your body is controlled by your subconscious mind, which is very open to what you say. Use your subconscious to take charge. It only needs to be left to do its own work, free from fear-based suggestions and negative thoughts. Be firm and say "No" to all bad thoughts, then shake them off. Leaving nature alone is the best way to stay healthy.

Breathing Exercise

Find a quiet place as far as possible, where the air is pure and the surroundings soothing and pleasant. After a bath or a thorough rubbing of the body from top to toe, with a wet towel, on an empty stomach, take this exercise: Send a current of holy thought to everyone, on planes seen and unseen, north and south, east and west, engage in meditation--take anyone of the meditation exercises you like. When you are perfectly calm and relaxed, seat yourself cross-legged, assuming any posture that comes easiest to you, with head, neck and chest held in a straight line and the weight of the upper parts of the body resting on ribs. Keep the region about the waist quite free. Loosen the cloth there out and out. Now inhale air slowly and steadily through right nostril after closing left nostril with your finger as long as it takes to count sixteen mentally. Close both nostrils, holding the inspired air within and count sixty-four. Then very slowly exhale the air through the left nostril for as long as it takes to count thirty-two. You must begin with a 4 second inhalation, 16 second retention and 8 second exhalation. Instead of dry counting you might improve yourself decidedly by repeating the word "Fearless" as many times holding mentally that dominant idea back of the word. Practise 5 pranayamas mornings and evenings for one week daily. Increase to 10 next week. Work up to 20. Go slowly. Practise as long as you like, but not less than 6 months. Be serious and earnest. This is not for non-serious minds. This exercise will augment digestive power, steady heart-action, make the body light and the mind calm. It shall help also miraculously in your Soul-Unfoldment. During this practice be pure in all ways. Observe Bramhacharya. Practice mental concentration and spiritual meditation. Don't talk much with others. Don't encourage any but holy society. Don't sleep much. Don't work very hard. Keep your emotions well-in-hand. Be always engaged mentally and physically. Be hopeful and cheerful. Never encourage negative thinking. It shall do wonders for you.

Physical Exercise

Exercise 1

Face a corner of the room and stand straight with your feet about 14 or 15 inches from the corner. Your arms should be straight out, with your hands on the walls on either side of you, chest out and belly in. Don't move your feet or bend your knees as you lean forward towards the corner. Aim to lightly touch the corner with your chest while keeping your head and stomach as far away from the corner as you can. Let your arms and hands slide forward on the walls in a straight line with your shoulders. Go back to the first pose and do it again without moving your feet or lowering your arms. As you move forward slowly, take a slow, deep breath in through your nose. Then, stretch your chest forward and upward (be careful not to hit your head on the wall) and your head and abdomen backward, which will straighten your back at the shoulders. Hold the chest against the corner for a moment while holding your breath. Then, slowly stand back up while bowing your head forward towards your chest and slowly letting out your breath. As you lean forward towards the corner, count along in your head: one, two, three, etc. As you stand back up, let out a breath, and mentally bend your head forward, say to yourself, "I am fearless, pure, and strong." Always move these things very slowly, carefully, and with full attention. Start with 5 or 6 moves and work your way up to 20 at a time.

Exercise 2

Keep your back straight and stand two feet away from the wall. Hold your hands out in front of you, palms facing the wall. Without moving your feet or bending your body, slowly lean forward and breathe in as you do so until your chest hits the wall. Then, slowly push yourself back up, breathing out as you do so. Do it at least 10 times.

Exercise 3

Hold hands behind your back. As you slowly breathe in, slowly move the hand that is clasped down as far as you can. At the same time, straighten your arms at the elbows and drop your shoulders as much as you can. Lift your chest as high as you can. Hold your breath and the pose for a moment, with your shoulders down, your chest out and up, and your stomach in. Then, let go of your hand and slowly let out your breath. An workout that is pretty hard. Take it easy.

Exercise 4

Stand with your back straight, your arms out to the sides, and your head up. Tense the muscles in your right arm, slowly doubling at the elbow and hand until the clenched fist touches your shoulders. Tend the muscles in your neck, lift your chin, and slowly turn your head to face the clenched fist. Do it again with your left arm. From the shoulder to the elbow, the arms must stay flat on the ground.

Exercise 5

Keep your back straight and your hands by your sides. Slowly bend as far to the right as you can and then as far to the left as you can. Do it 10 times.

Exercise 6

Keep your arms at your sides and stand up straight. Stretch your body out to the right and lean as far forward as you can without moving your knees. Keep your arms and body as loose as possible. Do it five times. After that, roll five times to the left.

Exercise 7

Keep your back straight. Spread your arms out in front of you. Wave them back and forth, like swimming backwards, until they meet above your head. At the same time, slowly take a full breath in while leaning back as far as you can. Now, take a deep breath out and bend forward until your fingers touch your toes. Be careful not to bend your knees. Keep your head as low as possible and your toes and fingers as straight as possible. Repeat standing up straight. Always keep your knees straight. As you move your arms up, try to stretch your whole body and hands as far forward and backward as you can. No need to touch the floor if your knees are bent. Just get as close as you can. You'll get stronger until you can touch it with practice.

Exercise 8

Lay on your back on the floor with your hands clasped under your head. Tense the muscles in your right leg and slowly lift the knee until it touches or almost touches your body. At the same time, bend your foot as far down as you can and stretch your toes towards the floor. Slowly lower your right leg to the floor while keeping it tight. Make sure the knee is straight and the toe is facing up towards your body. Lift the left leg up in the same way as the right, tensing the muscles and bringing the knee to the chest while stretching the toes up. As the left leg goes down, point the toes and foot towards the knee five times, gradually building up to ten times.

Physical Exercises

Series 2

Exercise 1

Stand with your arms straight out in front of you, at shoulder height, with the palms of your hands touching. Swing your hands back until your arms are straight out to the side from your shoulders, or even further back if they can go there without any effort. Quickly return to position 1, and do this several times. It's important that the arms move quickly and with life and movement. Do not fall asleep over work; instead, play. This workout is best for building up the chest, shoulder, and other muscles. When swinging your arms backward, it's better if you stand on your toes during the backward sweep and sink down on your feet when you move your arms forward again. Backward and forward moves should be done in a rhythmic way, like a fast pendulum swinging back and forth.

Exercise 2

(1) Extend the arms straight in front of you, letting the little fingers of each hand touch each other, the palms being upward; (2) then keeping the little fingers still touching, bring the hands straight up in a curved circular movement, until the tips of the fingers of both hands touch the top of the head back of the forehead, the backs of the fingers touching, the elbows swinging out as the movement is made until (when the fingers touch the head, with thumbs pointing the rear) they point out straight sideways; (3) let the fingers rest on the top of the head a moment, and then with the elbows pressing back (which forces the shoulders back) force the arms backward with an oblique motion until they reach the sides at full length, as in the standing position.

Exercise 3

(1) Extend the arms straight out, sideways, from the shoulders; (2) then, still keeping the upper arms extended in same position, bend the arms at the elbow and bring the forearm upward with a circular movement, until the tips of the extended fingers

lightly touch the tops of the shoulders; (3) then with fingers in the last position, force the elbows out to the front until they touch, or nearly go (a little practice will enable you to touch them together); (4) then, keeping the fingers still lightly touching the tops of the shoulders, swinging the elbows as far back as you can get them. (A little practice will enable you to get them much farther back than at the first attempt.) (S) Swing the elbows to the front position and then back to the rear position, several times.

Exercise 4

(1) Place the hands on the hips, thumbs to the rear, and elbows pressed back; (2) bend the body forward, from the hips as far as you can, keeping the chest protruding and the shoulders pressed back; (3) raise the body to the original standing position (hands still at the hips) and then bend backward. In these movements the knees should not be bent and the motions should be made slowly and gently; (4) then (hands still on the hips) bend gently to the right, keeping the heels firmly on the ground, knees unbent and avoid twisting the body; (5) resume original position, and then bend the body gently to the left, observing the precautions given in the last movement. This exercise is somewhat fatiguing and you should be careful not to overdo it at the start. Proceed gradually; (6) with hands in same position on the hips, swing the upper part of the body around in a circle, from the waist-up, the head describing the largest circle, of course. Do not move the feet or bend the knees.

Exercise 5

(1) Standing erect, with hands on hips, raise yourself on the balls of the feet several times, with sort of a springing motion. Pause a moment after you have raised upon your toes, then let the heels sink to the floor, then repeat, as above suggested. Keep the knees unbent and the heels together. This exercise is specially beneficial in developing the calf of the leg, and will make it sure the first few times it is tried. If you have an undeveloped calf here is the exercises for you; (2) with hands still on hips place your feet about two feet apart, and then cover the body into a "squatting" position, pausing a moment and then resuming original position. Repeat several times, but not too often at the first, as it will make the thighs feel a little sore at the beginning. This exercise will give one well developed thighs. This last movement may be improved upon by sinking down with the weight resting upon the balls of the foot, instead of upon the heel.

Exercise 6

(1) Stand erect with hands on hips; (2) keeping the knee straight, swing the right leg out about fifteen inches (keeping the toe turned a little out and the sole flat)--then swing back to the rear until the toe points straight to the ground, keeping the knee stiff all the time; (3) repeat the swinging backward and forward several times; (4) then do the same with the left leg; (5) with hands still on hips, raise the right leg up, bending the knee, until the upper-leg (thigh)

stands straight out from the body (if you can raise it still higher, you may do so); (6) place your foot again on the ground, and go through the same motion with the left leg; (7) repeat several times, first one leg and then the other, moving slowly at first and gradually increasing your speed until you are executing a slow trot without moving from the over spot.

Exercise 7

(1) Stand erect, with the arms extended straight in front of you, from the shoulders, and of course on a level with the shoulders--the palms must be down, fingers straight out, thumbs folded under and the thumb side of hands touching each other; (2) bend the body forward from the hips, stooping forward as far as possible and at the same time swing the arms forward with a sweeping movement, sending them down, backward and upward at the back, so that when the body has reached the limit of the bending forward movement the arms are extended back and over the body--keep the arms stiff and do not bend the knees; (3) resume standing position and repeat several times.

Exercise 8

(1) Extend the arms straight, sideways, from the shoulder and hold them there stiff and rigid with hands open; (2) close the hands forcibly with a quick motion, pressing the fingers well into the palm; (3) open the hands forcibly and quickly, spreading out the fingers and thumbs as widely as possible forming

a fan shaped hand; (4) close and open the hands as above stated, several times, as rapidly as possible. Put life into the exercise. This is a splendid exercise for developing the muscles of the hand and for acquiring manual dexterity.

Exercise 9

(1) Lie upon your stomach, extending your arms above your head and then bowed upward and your legs stretched out full length and raised backward and upward. The correct position may be carried in the mind by imagining a watch-crystal or a saucer resting on the table on its middle, with both ends turning upward; (2) lower and raise the arms and legs, several times; (3) then turn over on your back and lie extended at full length, with arms extended straight out upwards over the head, with back of fingers touching the ground; (4) then raise up both legs from the waist until they stand straight up in the air, like the mast of a ship, your upper-body and arms remaining in the last position named. Lower the legs and raise them several times; (5) resume position 3, lying flat upon the back at full with arms extended straight out upward, over the head, with backs of fingers touching the ground; (6) then gradually raise body to sitting position, with arms projecting straight in front of the shoulders. Then go back gradually to the lying down position, and repeat the raising and lowering several times; (7) then turn over on the face and stomach again and assume the following position:--Keeping the body rigid from head to foot, raise your body until its weight rests upon your palms (the arms being stretched out straight in front

of you) at one end, and upon your toes at the other end. Then gradually bend arms at the elbow, allowing your chest to sink to the floor; then raise up your chest and upper-body by straightening out your arms, the entire weight falling upon the arms, with the toes as a pivot--this last is a difficult motion, and should not be overdone at first.

Exercise 10

This exercise is for those troubled with a too large abdomen, which trouble is caused by too much fat gathering there. The abdomen may be materially reduced by a reasonable indulgence in this exercise--but always remember "moderation in all things" and do not overdo matters, or be in too much of a hurry. Here is the exercise: (1) exhale the breath (breathe out all the air in the lungs, without straining yourself too much) and then draw the abdomen in and up as far as you can, then hold for a moment and let it resume its natural position. Repeat a number of times and then take a breath or two and rest a moment. Repeat several times, moving it in and out. It is surprising how much control one may gain over these stubborn muscles with a little practice. This exercise will not only reduce the fatty layers over the abdomen, but will also greatly strengthen the stomach muscles. (2) Give the abdomen a good but not rough kneading and rubbing.

Exercise 11

The exercise is as follows:-Follow it carefully. (1) stand erect, with heels together, toes slightly pointed outward; (2) raise the arms up by the sides (with a circular movement) until the hands meet over the head, thumbs touching each other; (3) keeping the knees stiff; the body rigid; the elbows unbent; (and shoulders bent well back as the movement is made); bring down the hands, slowly, with a sideway circular motion, until they reach the sides of the legs the little finger and the inner-edge (the "chopping-edge") of the hand alone touching the legs, and palms of the hands facing straight to the front. The shoulder gets the right position by touching the little finger of each hand to the seam of the trousers. (4) Repeat several times, slowly remember. With the hands in the last position, having been placed there by the motion stated, it is very difficult for the shoulders to warp forward. The chest is projected a little; the head is erect; neck is straight, the back straight and hollowed a little (the natural position); and the knees are straight. In short, you have a fine, erect carriage-now keep it.

Seven Minor Breathing Exercises

Exercise 1

(1) Stand erect with hands at sides. (2) Inhale complete breath.

Raise the arms slowly, keeping them rigid until the hands touch over head. (4) Retain the breath a few minutes with hands over head. (5) Lower hands slowly to sides exhaling slowly at the same time. (6) Practise cleansing breath.

Exercise 2

(1) Stand erect with arms straight in front of you. (2) Inhale complete breath and retain. (3) Swing arms back as far as they will go; then back to first position; then repeat several times, retaining the breath all the while. (4) Exhale vigorously through mouth. (5) Practise cleansing breath.

Exercise 3

(1) Stand erect with arms straight in front of you. (2) Inhale complete breath. (3) Swing arms around in a circle, backward, a few times. Then reverse a few times retaining the breath all the while. You may vary this by rotating them alternately like the sails of a wind-mill. (4) Exhale the breath vigorously through the mouth. (5) Practise cleansing breath.

Exercise 4

(1) Lie on the floor with your face downward, and palms of hands flat upon the floor by your sides. (2) Inhale complete breath and retain. (3) Stiffen the body and raise yourself up by the strength of your arms until you rest on your hands and toes. (4) Then lower yourself to original position. Repeat several times. (5) Exhale vigorously through the mouth. (6) Practise cleansing breath.

Exercise 5

(1) Stand erect with your palms against the wall. (2) Inhale complete breath and retain. (3) Lower the chest to the wall, resting your weight on your hands. (4) Then raise yourself back with the arm muscles alone, keeping the body stiff. (5) Exhale vigorously through the mouth. (6) Practise cleansing breath.

Exercise 6

(1) Stand erect with arms "akimbo" that is with hands resting around the waist and elbows standing out. (2) Inhale complete breath and retain. (3) Keep legs and hips stiff and bend well forward, as if bowing, at the same time exhaling slowly. (4) Return to first position and then take another complete breath. (5) Then bend backward exhaling slowly. (6) Return to first position and take a complete breath. (7) Then bend sideways exhaling slowly (vary by bending to right and then to left). (8) Practise cleansing breath.

Exercise 7

(1) Stand erect or sit erect with straight spinal column. (2) Inhale a complete breath but instead of inhaling on a continuous steady stream, take a series of short, quick "sniffs" as if you were smelling aromatic salts and ammonia and did not wish to get too strong a "whiff." Do not exhale any of these little breaths, but add one to the other until the entire lung space is filled. (3) Retain for a few seconds. (4) Exhale through the nostrils in a long restful breath. (5) Practise cleansing breath.

During Training

Do not attempt to take all the above exercises at one and the same time. Take them several times in the day. Never exercise immediately after a meal or before it. Do not try to force development as you will be apt to suffer from re-action. Slow and steady wins the race. Gentle and persistent exercises are advisable. That will lead to permanent development.

Effect of Mind and Body

Even in the real world, it has been proven beyond a doubt that "what a man thinketh in his heart, so is he." Fear and worry thoughts are bad things to think about. These and all other bad feelings are partly caused by bad health, but it's even more true that bad health is caused by bad thinking. Fear changes the heart. During outbreaks like cholera, plague, etc., you frequently first project the harmful germs of fear-thoughts onto yourself. This weakens your mind, which in turn weakens your body and leaves you open to disease. If you believe negative advice from people who don't know what they're talking about and keep telling yourself that a certain disease has taken up residence in you and made your body its "fixed abode," you will die faster. Both the body and the mind are linked. Your thoughts become real in your body. Stay as far away from thoughts of sickness, old age, and weakness as possible and keep health-related thoughts in your mind at all times. The only way to really protect yourself from getting sick is to deny that sickness has any power over you. Say things like, "I can't be sick" or "I won't admit I'm sick." The strong will is what makes you healthy and strong. Free yourself from the belief that God sends sickness. You own your body and should take care of it. God will give you the power to control your body; in fact, He already has. Always keep in mind that you are the only one who can save yourself. You have the ability to hold all power and wisdom. Have faith in what you're doing and get it going. Keep working at it, and it will grow and unfold. You are in God and God is in you. When you pray, you're just helping that Latent Power unwind itself, even if you're not aware of it. Remember that God will give you the chance, the tools, the knowledge, and the power to do something, but you will have to do it yourself. So, as you can see, having a clear mind is very important for good health. Get rid of any weak ideas you have. Keep your thoughts strong. Finally, remember:

Mind acts Upon Body in all ways

Think good thoughts about your body. That's what I told you to do. Working out your body and your mind together will help you get Power and Poise. Along with this come health laws. But remember that your mind and body will have to do what you say if you use your power over them in private. It's like the body has its own mind. This intelligence is very good at what it does. That's what you call instinct. It breaks down food, moves trash out of the body, heals wounds, works the heart and controls circulation, and oversees all the other natural and automatic processes in the body. This instinctive mind is very good at what it does. You should know that the intelligence in your body's cells and nerve centres is opposite to the "I Am" (Central Intelligence) intelligence in your brain, which is in charge. Your brain's ideas, beliefs, and thoughts can change this intelligence. To stop releasing bad thoughts from your mind, all you have to do is leave it alone. If, on the other hand, you break the Laws of Nature and mess up the Instinctive Mind's work, you will get sick. Disease is just nature's way of getting rid of unnatural situations and restoring natural ones. In this case, all that needs to be done is to return to normal states. To do this, all you have to do is make your body healthier and change the way you think. Take the "belief" that your stomach is weak, your heart is weak, your liver is slow, your circulation is bad, your vitality is low, etc., for example. Your mind will quickly take up these beliefs and work them out literally. The Instinctive Mind, which is the same thing as the body's sub-conscious Mind, never thinks about what's right or wrong. It's on the level of automatism. So, if you've been thinking negatively like this, the first thing you should do is use Positive Denial to get rid of these unwanted mental weeds. Hold your breath and say, "No, No, No. My body is strong. My stomach is strong, my heart is strong, etc." Here, you use both positive denial and positive affirmation to make your point. If used correctly, the first one destroys evil, while the second one creates good. Belief and expecting the best are powerful things. Make sure you use them right. Mind has the most power over matter, and this has been proven.

Reserve Force

I want to draw your attention to the Reserve Power that is already inside you. Without a doubt, you have soul-powers that will come to life in a brilliant way when you are able to grow and expand your brain to the point where it can perfectly respond to your will. Really, your will, which is the divine part of you, is always strong and must unfold "as a rose" by working out in the fields of matter, force, and mind. These are all under YOUR control, and the real goal of human evolution is to give YOU the power wand.

There is a natural counterpart to everything that is going on inside your body. Take charge of nature inside, and you'll be able to move through the world like a master.

Now, without going into too much detail, let me tell you—if you don't already know this—that mind is the purest form of matter and matter is the grossest form of mind. The two are always interacting with each other. But mind can control matter because mind is the positive end and matter is the negative end. By giving a stimulus to the edge, you can bring about states of consciousness. Again, mental states cause vibrations in the cells of the body and brain that are similar to those in the state of consciousness.

So, you can see that your mind shapes and controls your body. Another way that your body affects your mind is through the part of your mind that works through your brain, which is just matter. So, to keep the polarities of your brain and body in balance, you need to keep adjusting the forces. This is how you can achieve POISE.

There are two things that must always be true in order to be in perfect health. The sickness has no power over you. There is health in a strong will. Disease and death are in the thoughts of someone who is weak, unstable, and afraid. At the same time, always be in sync with the physical rules of health. Knowing this and becoming less afraid of things will help you express yourself physically and mentally in ways you haven't thought of before. Sincere researchers in the field of physiology have come to the inevitable conclusion that there is a finely tuned, constantly changing substance that holds the reorganisation together, promotes growth, vigour, and motion, heals injuries, makes up for losses, and defeats and cures diseases. It was called "Archeus" by Von Helment and "Anima" by Stahl. It was known as the "sentiment principle" by Whytt. It was called "Caloric" by Dr. Cullen. Many people have named it different things, like "Vital Principle," "Living Power," "Conservative Power," "Odic Force," and so on. Dr. Darwin called it "Sensorial energy," and Rush called it "Occult Cause." We Indians know about it and have come up with Yoga techniques to control it. We call it

Prana, and you can only find guys in India who have pranic control, or control over universal energy.

In your body, there are reserve stores of vital energy ready to be used. These are mostly in the central ganglion of your vital battery, which is called the Solar Plexus, and in the chain of ganglia, or storage batteries, that run along and up your spine and in other nerve centres. The solar plexus is also called the "abdominal brain," and the energy for your brain comes from this important area. You will feel this part of your body (at the back of your stomach) getting warmer after a long time of focus and brain work. You must have noticed that when you work out, for example, you get tired and all worked up pretty quickly. But if you wait a little while and then start again, you will notice that you are not as tired and that you can run your body hard for a long time. The more you work out, the stronger and more powerful the surge of vital energy you feel. It seems like each new effort gives you a fresh start. Physiologists don't understand this. In brain work, you will find a similar thing. You might feel tired and worn out when doing brain-work that requires a lot of focus and close attention, but if you go back to your work a little while later, you will be able to do it with a surprising amount of freshness, vigour, and enthusiasm that far exceeds your first try. Again, anyone can and does use universal energy when they feel like they have to in an emergency situation that will surprise even themselves. Regardless of who you are or how healthy you are, your body has a huge amount of power that has never been used and is eagerly awaiting its wake-up call. Going at a normal dog trot speed, stopping to rest and limp while "taking care of our health," we feel like we're doing our best. Make sure you don't let your mind trick you into thinking you are "tired" and "old." Neither of them is true except in your own mind. You don't have any powers at the moment. Your hidden powers are all sitting there unused. In the background of your mind are huge energies that are ready for you to pull them out. When your brain thinks of being something incredibly great, or at least that's how it seems from your point of view, don't doubt your strength; instead, go ahead without hesitation, without fear, and calmly. Show your life power. Think of yourself as young, strong, healthy, and fit. Think of yourself as strong all the time and never think of yourself as weak. Hold on tight and run straight ahead. Nature will follow your plan. The great outdoors will always give you strength, energy, and vigour. You friends who write me that "there is a serious lack of vitality" in your system makes it impossible for you to deal with the occult should try this. Not like that. You really don't have any guts, initiative, pluck, or "go," and your thoughts are holding you back. If you change the way you think, your backup forces will come out and do something. You'll be a different person in no time.

How To Exercise

When you work out, try to find a rhythm of movements. Make sure your moves are smooth, easy, regular, and rhythmic. Pay attention to your work. Pay attention. Mind and Willpower should go into your work. Think about what it means. Do not wear yourself out too much. Towelling off or taking a spray bath is a good idea after working out. After you wet the towel, rub your body all over with it. Lift the towel and do it again. You should have a great glow after working out and drying off. When you work out, make sure the windows are open. You have to get some fresh air. Don't worry about being cold and other things. Don't forget that positive denial will give you the power to fight back. Say to yourself, "Cold can't hurt me," and mean it. You can deal with anything this way and not change.

Bathing and Linen

Every day, the student should take a bath with lots of water and rub and clean their whole body. I take cold water baths very early in the morning, all year round. Cold water improves circulation and is a great tonic for the body and the skin. Warm water has a calming effect on the body. Even better is taking a bath in the moving water of a river. Swimming is a great way to strengthen your bones and is also fun. Prana is in water, and your body gets it from food, drink, and the air. Since this isn't a "doctor" book, I can't tell you how to bathe in different ways. If you can, take a bath twice a day, in the morning and at night. If you can't, just bathe once in the morning and use a towel the rest of the time. Bathing is more than just putting water on your body; you clean it from top to bottom by rubbing and scrubbing it with water and your hands and towels. Try to be as clean as possible. It is said that cleanliness is godliness and health is holiness.

Let the water flow over your body again while you bathe and try to "appreciate the sensation" and think about how water absorbs Prana. This will help you twice as much.

About Linens: Please clean up. Many times a day, these religious people wash their hands and take two baths, but their clothes are still dirty, sweaty, and oily. No matter what else it may mean, religion does not mean filth, bad smells coming from your body and clothes, and ignoring clean clothing and dirt on the outside. The Yogi is the most FINE person in the world. Read that word and know what it means. You shouldn't wear day clothes at night. Be clean on the inside and the outside. Clean up. Clean up. Be clean on the inside and the outside.

Drinking Water and Swallowing Air

Your body needs a good amount of air and water. Nature does many things with water. A good habit is to drink 5 to 8 tumblers of clean water every day. Imagine that your Prana is being absorbed by the water as you drink it slowly.

The student also needs a lot of fresh air. If your heart and lungs are healthy, they will automatically take in air and release oxygen in the right amounts. Unless you already do them, do these movements carefully one at a time outside every day. You can count on them.

The Yogi Cleansing Breath

(1) Inhale a complete breath. (2) Retain the air a few seconds. (3) Pucker up the lips as if for a whistle (but do not swell out the cheeks) then exhale a little air through the opening with considerable vigor. Then stop for a moment retaining the air and then exhale a little more air. Repeat until the air is completely exhaled. Remember that considerable vigor is to be used in exhaling air through the opening in the lips. This breath will be found quite refreshing when one is tired and generally "used up." A trial will convince the student of its merits. This exercise should be practised until it can be performed naturally and easily, as it is used to finish up a number of other exercises given in this book and it should be thoroughly understood.

Nerve Vitalising Breath

(1) Stand erect. (2) Inhale a complete breath and retain same. (3) Extend the arms straight in front of you, letting them somewhat limp and relaxed, with only sufficient nerve force to hold them out. (4) Slowly draw the hands back towards the shoulders gradually, contracting the muscles and putting force into them, so that when they reach the shoulders the fists will be so tightly clenched that a tremulous motion is felt. (5) Then keeping the muscles tense push the fists slowly out and then draw them back rapidly (still tense) several times. (6) Exhale vigorously through the mouth. (7) Practise the cleansing breath. (8) The efficiency of this exercise depends greatly upon the

speed of the drawing back of the fists, and the tension of the muscles, and, of course upon the full lungs. This exercise must be tried to be appreciated. It is without equal as a "bracer" as our western friends put it.

The Vocal Breath

(1) Inhale a complete breath very slowly, but steadily, through the nostrils, taking as much time as possible in the inhalation. (2) Retain for a few seconds. (3) Expel the air vigorously in one great breath, through the wide-opened mouth. (4) Rest the lungs by the cleansing breath. This would give you a good, rolling voice.

The Retained Breath

(1) Stand erect. (2) Inhale a complete breath. (3) Retain the breath as long as you can comfortably. (4) Exhale vigorously through the open mouth. (5) Practise the cleansing breath. At first you will be able to retain the breath only a short time, but a little practise will also show a great improvement. Time yourself with a watch, if you wish to note your progress.

Cell Stimulation

(1) Stand erect with hands in sides. (2) Breathe in very slowly and gradually. (3) While inhaling, gently tap the chest with the fingertips, constantly changing position. (4) When the lungs are filled, retain the breath and

the chest with the palms of the hands. (5) Practise the cleansing breath.

Rib Stretching

(1) Stand erect. (2) Place the hands one on each side of the body as high up in the armpits as convenient, the thumbs reaching towards the back, the palms on the side of the chest and the fingers to the front over the breast. (3) Inhale a complete breath. (4) Retain the air for a short time. (5) Then gently squeeze the sides at the same time slowly exhaling. (6) Practise the cleansing breath.

Chest Expansion

(1) Stand erect. (2) Inhale a complete breath. (3) Retain the air. (4) Extend both arms forward and bring the two clenched fists together on a level with the shoulder. (5) Then swing back the fists vigorously until the arms stand out straight side-ways from the shoulders. (6) Then bring back to position (4) and swing to position (5). Repeat several times. (7) Exhale vigorously through the open mouth. (8) Practise the cleansing breath.

Walking Exercise

(1) Walk with head up, chin drawn slightly in, shoulders back, and with measured tread. (2) Inhale a complete breath, counting (mentally) 1,2, 3, 4, 5, 6, 7, 8, one count to each step making the inhalation extend

over the eight counts. (3) Exhale slowly through the nostrils, counting as before 1, 2, 3, 4, 5, 6, 7, 8, one count to a step. (4) Rest between breaths, continuing, walking and counting 1, 2, 3, 4, 5, 6, 7, 8, one count to a step. (5) Repeat until you begin to feel tired. Then rest for a while and resume at pleasure. Repeat several times a day. You may vary the exercise by retaining the breath during a 1,2, 3, 4, count and then exhale in an eight-step count. Practise whichever plan seems most agreeable to you.

Morning Exercise

(1) Stand erect in a military attitude, head up, eyes front, shoulders back, knees stiff, hands at sides. (2) Raise body slowly on toes, inhaling a complete breath, steadily and slowly. (3) Retain the breath for a few seconds, maintaining the same position. (4) Slowly sink the first position at the same time slowly exhaling the air through the nostrils. (5) Practise cleansing breath. (6) Repeat several times, varying by using right leg alone, then left leg alone.

Stimulating Circulation

(1) Stand erect. (2) Inhale a complete breath and retain. (3) Bend forward slightly and grasp a stick or cane steadily and firmly, and gradually exerting your entire strength upon the grasp. (4) Relax the grasp, return to first position, and slowly exhale. (5) Repeat

several times. (6) Finish with the cleansing breath. (N. B. The above are from the Yoga Teachings.)

Meditation Exercise 1

Get away from the noise. Say, "I AM NOT AFRAID." Think about that idea in a calm way. You should think about it in every way. See yourself in your thoughts as having the quality you want and then act it out in real life. Take some time to daydream about something very dramatic. Just make sure it sticks to the specific text of thought and always shows you as a winner in the end. Close with a strong declaration of "I am." Do it every day at the same time for at least six months.

Exercise 2

Get away from the noise. Focus your mind on this: "I send strong, positive, healing thought waves of love to everyone." Let those who are sick get better. Help the weak get stronger. Let those who are in need get rich and happy. Help the ones who are scared to become brave. Those who are mean should change and be kind. Let the people who hate and hurt others learn to love. Let those who aren't pure become pure. Please calm and soothe those who have lost a loved one or are feeling sad.

Think of strong waves of Thought-Force coming from you and going around the whole world. Imagine that the world is full of men and women who are making the conditions you want happen.

As was said above, it's better for friends to sit together and focus on the union of will and mind. Work out by yourself if you can't find anyone else who is also sincere and serious.

Believe that you can help people in this way. You can think anything and it will happen. Blessing others is a way to bless yourself. There will be a lot of effects from this practice. It will come after and be a blessing to you even after you die. As much as possible, practise every day at the same time and place.

Do your work with all your heart.

Do not tell other people about your workouts.

Anyone who does the routines above will get stronger and better in a great way. You have already been shown how to do Pranayama, which means "controlling the psychic breath." The main thing it does is give you power over your Prana and bring out your psychic force. If you do it on a dirty body or lungs that aren't strong, it could hurt you. So, students should start with the 10 breathing exercises listed above. Once their lungs have built up the stamina to handle that, they should move on to it. It's going to take time, patience, and hard work. But if the student works hard enough, he will be able to do all of these tasks perfectly in six months. But go with the flow of nature and move slowly and steadily.

Diet

You all know that pure food brings pure blood. You should avoid the two extremes of gluttony and daily fasting and abstemiousness. You should know (1) What to eat (2) How to eat (3) When to eat.

Food that is concentrated and has the most nutrients in the least amount of food should be used. The student should get a good book on the relative values of foods and then use his own judgement. We eat nuts, milk, fruits, whole wheat bread, very little rice, beans, nuts, peanuts, etc. It is very important for people who don't eat meat to make sure that their meal has a lot of albuminous foods. This is because vegetarians often eat too many starchy foods and not enough nitrogenous foods.

Properly chew and masticate the food to get all of the Prana out of it and break it up into very small pieces, turning it into mush. Do not rush to swallow your food. Instead, let it stay in your mouth for a while so that your tissues can properly dry out and so that the nerves in your tongue, cheek, etc. can receive energy from the food. Don't forget that your gut doesn't have rows of teeth on it. This will give you twice as much energy as you normally do, keep you from getting constipated, and keep you from not absorbing enough food or eating too much. By getting the right amount of nutrition from a small amount of food, you can avoid "stuffing" your stomach with food that it doesn't need. It is also cheap, in case you are a thrifty person! Eat to stay alive. Don't eat to live.

When you're hungry, eat. That artificial "appetite" that wants to be satisfied at certain times of the day and makes you feel "all-gone" and sick to your stomach is not real "hunger." In real hunger, there is no feeling in the stomach, but there is a constant flow of saliva in the mouth, which makes you enjoy even the simplest foods. It will taste as sweet as Manna even if the bread crust is dry. Stop having breakfast. Instead, drink cold water. At noon, eat a nice, healthy meal. In the evening, eat something light.

Finally, kids, remember to live simply and think deeply. Don't be afraid to eat when you're hungry. Two square meals a day are fine as long as you work out and use your brain and body. Be careful not to become too light and airy, or you won't be useful in the world's work. When it comes to Brahmacharies, students won't care nearly as much about lots of food as regular people do. There is a steady sense of satisfaction and fullness in such. But hard workers should never show up like that. But people who work hard should never be hungry, and they need more food than others.

Sleep

Things that matter are how deep and calm your sleep is. People who are easily tense can't calm down and keep tossing at night. When it's hot, wash your feet in cold water. When it's cold, wash them in cool water. That will get rid of the extra blood that is gurgling in your head. Also, wash the back of your neck. As the student goes to sleep, he or she should meditate because while asleep, the Man leaves the physical form and goes to super-physical planes. Your last thought determines and shapes you into the special super-physical impact you want to achieve. There will also be great perks for your body. In this way, you will feel more relaxed, and your sleep will be better and more restful than without it. A good night's sleep is one of the most important signs that you have good Mental and Physical Control.

You are quiet and relaxed while you sleep, and all kinds of things happen around you that you can't see. So, putting yourself inside an Astral Shell is a good idea. Focus on your energy and picture it as a shell that goes 18 inches around you. To clear your thoughts, think about this affirmation.

I. I am charging my aura with my Will-Force.

II. It is strong, strong, strong and can and will resist, repel and drive off all bad influences and admit only pure and holy influence.

III. It will remain around me right along the period of my sleep.

The student is told to wrap himself in this "auric shell" even when he is awake so that it can protect him from all bad thoughts. Other people will be able to feel a Protective Aura around him as his Will-Power and Self-Confidence grow.

Relaxation Versus Contraction

The student should learn to relax his body completely so that it shall lie still and limp and soft as cotton. He should be able to tense and contract his muscles so that they will become hard as iron. In all the physical exercises you will find two special actions (1) Muscle contraction (2) Stretching. When you contract muscle and harden it, you have sent currents of nerve-force and will to that part; when you relax it, you "let go" completely. What we want is Strength in Repose ready to leap into action in the flash of an eye. We have taught you how to relax in Lesson 2 on Will-Force. You all have noticed a cat crouching for its prey. How intensely still it is; yet you know what such stillness means. It is very far from laziness. Relaxation husbands and conserves nerve-force. It is a great thing to be calm and silent. Calmness is the centralization of tremendous power. Practise being calm, as far as you can.

Solar Energy

Electricity and heat are both very powerful in the sun's rays. If a person's body were properly exposed to the sun for five hours in the morning and five hours at night, it would gain strength and store energy. Do not do this too much, especially if you live in a warm place.

Last word on Health

Faith in Nature. Your body-machine will be in great shape thanks to her office. A lot of people say,

"Prevention is better than cure." Look at the man who is healthy. Look at how he lives and try to live like him. Keep in mind, though, that you are in charge of your body and not God. Also, get rid of the stupid idea that God sends sickness. You will understand what Health Laws are if you think, study, and pay attention.

Conclusion

Dear Student, I have drawn the lines that you should follow to find your way to spiritual independence. I can't take care of your business, fix your problems, or do your work. I've given you some guidelines; pay attention, think, and learn everything you can. To reach your goals and become perfect, you have to go up the steps of the ladder of growth.

Fear is a big thing that gets in the way. Put it down. Make it go without food. Be sincere. Do everything. Be serious and quiet as you live your life. Offer to help others whenever you can, but don't do it with that condescending air of superiority that modern snobs wear as "gentlemen." You should be proud to be "Indian." Follow Indian ideas about how to be great. Think of it as an honour to help people who deserve it. In some way, we all need help, support, and direction. Cooperation and depending on each other are basic building blocks of human well-being. Keep going. Be a man. Have guts. Do good and great things. Add your voice to the growth of evolution around the world and help turn the wheel of life. When you help other people, you will also be helped in every area of your life. Don't be crazy. Be fair and just to other people. Help other people by being a blessing. Negative thoughts will keep stopping you from moving forward as long as they are bothering you. I've already told you "how" to move forward.

God bless you. May he lead, assist, and strengthen me where I have failed.

References

Dewey, J. 1981. The Later Works, 1925-1953: John Dewey. Vol. 1 Of 1925 Experience and Nature. Carbondale: Southern Illinois University Press.

Iyengar, B. K. S., J. J. Evans, and D. Abrams. 2006. Light on Life: The Yoga Journey to Wholeness, Inner Peace, and Ultimate Freedom. Pennsylvania: Rodale Books.

Jois, K. P. 1996. Ashtanga Yoga with Sri K. Pattabhi Jois. DVD. Los Angeles: Yoga Works Productions.

Kono, T. 2013. "Advantage of Participatory Research." [Tojisha Kenkyu no Yuisei]. In Tojisha Kenkyu no Kenkyu [Study of a Participatory Study], edited by K. Ishihara, 73-111. Tokyo: Igakushoin.

Kuwayama, K., M. Koseki, and M. Suwa. 2018. "The Story of Remains" [Ato no

Monogatari]. The 32nd Annual Conference of the Japanese Society for Artificial Intelligence. doi:10.11517/pjsai.JSAI2018.0_2B3OS19b02.

Nishigaki, T. 2018. AI Genron; Kami no Shihai to Ningen no Jiyu [AI Principles: Rule of God and Human Freedom]. Tokyo: Kodansha.

Polanyi, M. 1983. The Tacit Dimension. Gloucester, MA: Peter Smith.

Shusterman, R. 1997. Practicing Philosophy: Pragmatism and the Philosophical Life. 1st ed. New York: Routledge.

Shusterman, R. 2000a. Performing Live: Aesthetic Alternatives for the Ends of Art. 1st ed. New York: Cornell University Press.

Shusterman, R. 2000b. Pragmatist Aesthetics: Living Beauty, Rethinking Art. 2nd ed. New York: Rowman & Littlefield Publishers.

Shusterman, R. 2002. "Somaesthetics and Education." Bulletin of the Graduate School of Education, Hiroshima University Part 1 Learning and Curriculum Development 51: 17-24. doi:10.15027/16157.

Shusterman, R. 2010. "What Pragmatism Means to Me: Ten Principles." Revue Frangaise D'etudes Americaines 124: 59-65. doi:10.3917/rfea.124.0059.

Shusterman, R. 2012. Thinking through the Body: Essays in Somaesthetics. New York: Cambridge University Press.

Shusterman, R. 2019. "Somaesthetic Practice and the Question of Norms." In Questions of Practice in Philosophy and Social Theory, edited by A. Buch and T. R. Schatzki, 136-153. Abingdon: Routledge.

Stephens, M. 2010. Teaching Yoga: Essential Foundations and Techniques. Berkeley: North Atlantic Books.

Suwa, M. 2008. "A Cognitive Model of Acquiring Embodied Expertise through

Meta-cognitive Verbalization." Transactions of the Japanese Society for Artificial Intelligence 23 (3): 141 -150. doi:10.1527/tjsai.23.141.

Suwa, M. 2016. Kotsu to Slump no Kenkyu: Shintaichi no Ninchikagaku [Research of Know-how and Slump: Cognitive Science of Embodied Knowledge]. Tokyo: Kodansha.

Varela, F., and J. Shear. 1999. "First-person Methodologies: What, Why, How?" Journal of Consciousness Studies 6 (2-3): 1-14.

Index

A

B

C

D

E

T

U

V

W

Y

9 789360 093419

Printed at Repro India Ltd.